Sports Illustrated

THE GREAT ONE

THE COMPLETE **WAYNE GRETZKY** COLLECTION

FOREWORD BY **MICHAEL FARBER**

FENN
M&S

Library and Archives Canada Cataloguing in Publication

The great one : the complete Wayne Gretzky collection / Sports Illustrated, ed.

ISBN 978-0-7710-8361-7

1. Gretzky, Wayne, 1961-. 2. Hockey players – Canada – Biography.

GV848.5.G78G74 2012   796.962092   C2012-902776-6

We acknowledge the financial support of the Government of Canada through
the Canada Book Fund and that of the Government of Ontario through the
Ontario Media Development Corporation's Ontario Book Initiative. We further
acknowledge the support of the Canada Council for the Arts and the Ontario
Arts Council for our publishing program.

Published simultaneously in the United States of America by
Fenn/McClelland & Stewart, a division of Random House of Canada Limited Ltd.,
P.O. Box 1030, Plattsburgh, New York 12901

Library of Congress Control Number: 2012937981

Typeset in Palatino by M&S, Toronto
Printed and bound in the United States of America

Fenn/McClelland & Stewart, a division of Random House of Canada Limited
One Toronto Street
Suite 300
Toronto, Ontario
M5C 2V6
www.mcclelland.com

1   2   3   4   5   16   15   14   13   12

Sports Illustrated

THE GREAT ONE

CONTENTS

FOREWORD

MICHAEL FARBER

WAYNE GRETZKY IS GONE, BUT HIS FINGERPRINTS ARE everywhere.

He is not in the game – he left a sorry situation in Phoenix in 2009 and is still owed millions by a forlorn franchise that became the ward of the NHL – but in so many ways he remains the game. Modern hockey pros are all the sons of 99, earning their swell livings in a business he reinvented. When the puck is dropped in Anaheim or south Florida or any place else with beach weather, you sense Gretzky. When a surprising trade is made, someone always says, "Even Wayne Gretzky got traded. Twice." And when a player goes on a scoring jag, even in this Dead Puck era, you instinctively look up Gretzky because he is the standard by which any forward will be judged until hell freezes over or Canada melts. Gretzky held or shared 61 records – 40 regular season, 15 playoff, six All-Star – when he retired in 1999. They all still stand. Records were made to be broken. Just not his, apparently.

With deference to the fabulous Sidney Crosby, who scored the most important goal in the most important game ever contested on Canadian ice in the 135-year history of the arena game, Gretzky remains the one name in the sport that reverberates beyond its boundaries.

If Crosby hosts *Saturday Night Live,* as Gretzky did, awkwardly, in 1989, then we will be happy to revisit the theory.

The advent of the truly "modern" NHL is generally dated to the 1967 expansion that spread the game beyond the so-called Original Six, but it begins in earnest with Gretzky. Walter and Phyllis's son was destined for greatness but no one could have guessed this slender boy from Brantford, Ont., would presage hockey's future. The 13-year, $124-million contract Alexander Ovechkin signed in 2008 with Washington? On his 18th birthday, in 1979, Gretzky signed a 21-year personal services deal with Peter Pocklington, who owned the Edmonton Oilers, then of the World Hockey Association. The dismantling of the 2010 Stanley Cup champion Chicago Blackhawks for economic reasons? Through no fault of his own, Gretzky and his Oilers traveled that road decades before the salary-cap era. Breaking faith with a city, a country and a player who had hand-delivered four Stanley Cups, Pocklington traded Gretzky to the Los Angeles Kings on Aug. 9, 1988, thus representing the moment the NHL flew off its axis. The deal led to expansion in nontraditional markets in the United States as surely as Gretzky opened up the previously fallow space behind the net. The headline on E.M. Swift's trade story in SPORTS ILLUSTRATED: Woe, Canada. Indeed. In 1988, the year of the Gretzky's last Cup with the Oilers, seven of 21 teams (33.3%) were based in Canada; before the Atlanta Thrashers relocated to once-abandoned Winnipeg for the 2011–12 season, six of 30 teams (20%) were based in hockey's homeland.

If Gretzky could not see hockey's tectonic shift through his tears on the day that remains a where-were-you-when moment for many Canadians…well, that might be the first time he had failed to anticipate something. Gretzky-vision. He always operated in the astral plane, a hockey avatar able to peer into the immediate future.

Tomas Sandström occasionally played on a line with Gretzky in Los Angeles. "Wayne would tell me O.K., in three seconds after I carry the puck over the blue line and curl, I want you to be along the boards, between the extended goal line and the face-off circle."

"'O.K. Why?'

"'Because that's when the puck'll get to you.'

"And," said Sandström, who told me this story more than 15 years ago, "that's exactly what happened."

ONE OF MY FAVORITE SI STORIES ABOUT GRETZKY DOES NOT appear in this collection. The reason? The subject of the story was Mario Lemieux, not Gretzky. In February 1989, with Lemieux in the midst of the career season in which he would score 85 goals and 199 points in 76 games, writer Austin Murphy made a 3,000-word case that Lemieux had surpassed Gretzky as the world's best player. (Gretzky would manage a mere 54 goals and 168 points with the Kings in 1988–89.) You could make a good argument about Lemieux's supremacy if you took a snapshot of the two centers that winter, and Murphy did, but he failed to convince managing editor Mark Mulvoy, once a distinguished SI hockey writer who had covered the 1972 Summit Series. Mulvoy grasped the Gretzkyian tides of history and went with the flow. He toned down some of

Murphy's fulsome praise for Mario and made sure the writer stressed that Lemieux could not rightfully join Gretzky on the top step of the hockey pantheon until he had won some Stanley Cups (as he would in 1991 and 1992 with the Penguins). Then Mulvoy added punctuation on the cover shot of Lemieux. The cover line read: AS GREAT AS GRETZKY?

Gretzky's introduction to SI readers had occurred in the Feb. 20, 1978 issue, in a story by Swift, the magazine's most accomplished Gretzkyologist. Gretzky was 16 then, as much of a personage as he was a person in his homeland. Swift tailed the phenom around the Ontario junior league. Gretzky would turn pro later that year, with the WHA's Indianapolis Racers, but that winter he was still a pimply-faced boy who was putting up what, in the embryonic days of the video game, can only be called pinball-like numbers. Swift borrowed from Longfellow's epic poem, Hiawatha, describing Gretzky as "learned in all the lore of old men." He also cast him as "Canada's answer to Steve Cauthen and Nadia Comaneci," a pair of contemporary prodigies who, at the time, were far more famous in the United States.

In context the analogy flattered Gretzky, but those other names echo only faintly today. Cauthen was named SI's Sportsman of the Year in 1977 and became the youngest jockey to win the Triple Crown in 1978. By the following year, however, Cauthen, who struggled to maintain his weight, was off to England, as temporal a figure on the North American sporting scene as a passing summer at dusk. Comaneci, the Romanian gymnast who had stunned the 1976 Montreal Olympics with the seven perfect scores of 10 and five medals (three of them gold), won two more golds at the boycotted 1980 Games but soon was gone from the mats as often happens with tween tumblers. Gretzky endured, and he thrived. He played for 21 seasons and only once, in his final year, with the New York Rangers, did he fail to average at least a point per game.

Gretzky was the SI's Sportsman of the Year in 1982, the second hockey player so honored, after Bobby Orr in 1970. Swift, again, tried to make sense of a season that seems to stretch the bounds of credulity even more now than it did then. He wrote: "Last season, at 21, Gretzky put together a year that no one in hockey had thought possible: 92 goals and 120 assists for 212 points in 80 games. These totals are so far beyond the previous records that they're difficult to put in perspective. It's as if some kid suddenly hit 78 home runs, passing 60 by mid-August. Our sense of history was offended. The NHL's second-leading scorer last season, Mike Bossy, had the fourth-highest point total (147) in league history, but he trailed Gretzky by 65 points. That's half a season's work for most big scorers. Nowadays a 65-point year is not far from locking up a spot on one of the league's season-ending All-Star teams, a statistical reminder of how sorely Gretzky is missed.

For many Canadians outside of Edmonton, however, memories of Gretzky are linked as closely to country as they are to his four Stanley Cups or his 31 individual NHL trophies. The Gretzky-to-Lemieux winner in the 1987 Canada Cup was a preserved-in-amber moment, maybe the most meaningful goal scored by a Canadian on home ice by someone not named Crosby. But the most hotly debated Gretzky moment internationally did not occur on the ice but on the bench, in Nagano 1998, the first time NHL players went to the Olympics. Marc Crawford had the game's greatest scorer at his disposal, but the coach bypassed him in a semifinal shootout in favor of such unlikely candidates as Ray Bourque and Brendan Shanahan. The knock on Gretzky always had been that he was mediocre on breakaways. By Gretzky's elevated standards, that critique might even have been fair. But a middling Gretzky was still a superior option. There was no one more capable of bending a moment to his will. He had earned the right to take one of those five shots against the Czech Republic's Dominik Hasek simply because he was Wayne Douglas Gretzky. Alas, the defining image of those Games remains of Gretzky on the bench, head hung in sorrow. He would, of course, tidy up the Olympic ledger as Team Canada executive director in Salt Lake City 2002. SI hockey columnist Kostya Kennedy even suggested that Gretzky come out of retirement and name himself to the team. Mercifully, Gretzky let Lemieux and Steve Yzerman do the heavy lifting as Canada ended an Olympic gold-medal drought of 50 years.

Gretzky is past 50 now. The sharp contours of his face have softened, of course, but he still carries his age and his name well, a constant in Canadian lives for almost four decades. (Only his hairstyle has continually changed; follicly, he is more Canada's Hillary Clinton than Steve Cauthen or Nadia Comaneci.) Gretzky could have just been a cottage industry after retiring as a player, Wayne Gretzky Inc., living off his accomplishments and image, but he was born with the hockey gene. His time in Phoenix, in management and as a coach, ultimately proved to be a failure. Then again, Babe Ruth struck out 1,330 times.

Anyway as we were saying, Gretzky is gone but is never far away. And now in these pages, he gains the blue line, curls, chooses his option and makes us young again.

LEARNED IN ALL THE LORE OF OLD MEN

BY E.M. SWIFT | FEBRUARY 20, 1978

*Hiawatha was Sault Ste. Marie's first legend, but in the late
1970s the town hero was a teen-aged hockey phenom
named Wayne Gretzky, who played with a maturity far
beyond his years*

(Photograph by Lane Stewart)

MORE THAN 7,000 PEOPLE – THE LARGEST HOCKEY CROWD of the season in Canada's capital – came to the Ottawa Civic Center one night last month to get to the bottom of a 16-year-old wunderkind who plays for the Sault Ste. Marie (Ont.) Greyhounds. His name is Wayne Gretzky. That's with a Zed-K-Y, please. The immigration guy fouled it up when his grandfather came over from Russia. In Peterborough the next night, the same thing happened: largest crowd of the year even though the last-place Greyhounds provided the opposition. The night after that, it was the same story in Hamilton: first sellout of the year for a Junior A game, and in a blizzard to boot, everyone out getting stuck in the snow to see some kid called The Great Gretzky, whom every paper in Ontario has hailed as the next Bobby Orr since he was eight years old, 4'4" and 70 pounds.

Gretzky is not just another star of the future. He is there, Canada's answer to Steve Cauthen and Nadia Comaneci, one of those rare youths who leapfrogs the stage where they speak of potential, whose talent is already front and center, which, incidentally, is the position he plays for the Greyhounds. Gretzky is only a rookie in the Ontario Junior A Major Hockey Association (OHA), a league in which the players range in age from 16 to 20, but he has exploded onto the Junior scene like no one since Guy Lafleur – and before that Orr. If Wayne Gretzky were never to play another hockey game, thousands of Canadian kids would remember him into their dotage. He is the stuff of their dream – that, lacking size, lacking strength, lacking speed, they, too, can somehow make it.

Gretzky did. He now is a wiry (read "skinny") 155 pounds spread over 5'11", but he should fill out enough to keep the pros happy. Gretzky describes his speed as "brutal" – meaning slower than slow. All the speed in the family went to his 14-year-old sister Kim, the Ontario Dominion champion in the 100-, 200- and 400-meter dashes and a good bet to represent Canada in the 1980 Olympics. Gretzky's shot is accurate, but far from overpowering. And if you expect to see him mucking it up in the corners, forget it. Still, without question, he is the most exciting Junior hockey player since Lafleur left Quebec City in 1971.

"They compare me to Orr and Lafleur, and that's very flattering," says Gretzky in his best "shucks, who, li'l-ol'-me? tone. "But basically, my style is different from anyone else's." True. Nevertheless, despite the qualifier, Gretzky lives quite comfortably with comparisons involving himself and Orr, Lafleur or any other superstar who comes to mind, including Cauthen. "We're both little runts who get a lot of publicity," Gretzky says of the latter.

Gretzky's talent is all in his head. "He's the smartest kid I've ever seen," says Fred Litzen, Sault Ste. Marie's one-eyed head scout who has seen a passel of talent over 40 years, even if he has missed half, as his friends suggest. Gretzky knows not only where everyone *is* on the ice, but he also knows where they're *going*. Uncanny anticipation, people call it.

While Gretzky's straight-ahead speed is something less than overwhelming, his mobility makes him nearly impossible to check, and his quickness – "Oh God, he's got terrific reflexes," says Litzen – makes him a superb forechecker in the mold of Bobby Clarke, the player after whom Gretzky models himself the most. Right now, Gretzky has a knack with the puck equal to anyone's, at any level. "From the red line to their net I play a solid game compared to anyone in the NHL," he says. And somehow such a statement from a 16-year-old does not have a cocky ring. It shouldn't, because it's true.

Defensively? Well, let's just say that one of the reasons Junior A hockey – the final step before the pros – is fun is that the games are often "Bombs-away LeMay" affairs. Gretzky does not return to his own zone to cover a man, he goes there only because without the puck he cannot start a rush. No one particularly worries about his defensive work, least of all Gretzky, who seems as aware as anyone that covering the opposing center is not apt to make headlines. As Greyhound Coach Muzz MacPherson says, "With a kid his age, you don't take away his puck sense and tell him to play defense. He's got plenty of time for that."

One reason for the big commotion over Gretzky last month was his play in the World Junior Championships that were held in and around Montreal over the Christmas holidays. The youngest player in the eight-nation field, Gretzky led all scorers with 17 points (eight goals, nine assists) in six games. Team Canada, however, finished a disappointing third, behind the Soviet Union and Sweden.

Gretzky was the host country's only representative on the all-tournament team and became, if not a national hero, something of a national curiosity in a hockey-mad nation.

Leading scorer at 16? Who is this Gretzky guy?

Dan Lucas, Gretzky's right wing in Sault Ste. Marie, was also paired briefly with him on Team Canada. "He would come in and boast to all those older guys how he was going to score four or five points against the Czechs or something," Lucas says. "I'd shake my head and think, 'What are you saying, kid?' Then he'd go out and get them. Unreal. I've had things go well for me before, but with him it never stops. If he ever has a comeuppance, it's going to be a dandy."

IT HAS BEEN THAT WAY PRETTY MUCH FOR GRETZKY SINCE he was five. That year he made the Brantford, Ontario novice All-Star team, a squad usually made up of 10- and 11-year-olds. That led to an interview with the local television station at age six, a Toronto *Globe and Mail* feature at eight, a film clip on national television at nine. His career as a media darling was rolling. At 11 he scored 378 goals in 68 games, including three in 45 seconds in the third period of a game in which Brantford trailed 3–0. The legend grew, far faster than the boy.

After being the third player selected in the midget draft held by the OHA last spring, Gretzky was expected to need time to adjust to the rougher, faster pace of the mother lode of North American hockey. He didn't. He scored a hat trick in his first game with Sault Ste. Marie, and has been at the top of the OHA scoring race ever since. In his first 48 games Gretzky had 54 goals and 87 assists for 141 points. He already has shattered the rookie record of 137 points in a season (68 games) and may well break the OHA record of 170 points now held by Mike Kaszycki of the New York Islanders.

From the day Walter Gretzky strapped skates on his 2½-year-old son Wayne and shoved him onto the flooded backyard rink, a comeuppance just hasn't been in the cards.

HARRY WOLFE IS THE VOICE OF THE SOO GREYHOUNDS. HE shouts at his microphone with such vengeance that his broadcasts can be comfortably listened to while, say, running a bath. "In 25 years in this business," says Harry in a quieter moment, "I have never seen a kid capture the imagination of the Canadian public like Wayne Gretzky."

Harry knows all about capturing imaginations. Ask him to rate Gretzky, and he's apt to tell you that the kid is the best Junior hockey player since Harvey Keck. That's K-E-C-K, and no immigration guy fouled the name up – he's part Indian. Plays for the Mekitina Purple Raiders. A professional scout once heard Harry talking about Harvey Keck and went so far as to get directions to Mekitina, which requires a dogsled and a clear night even in summer. A compass won't work that far north.

Keck's only weakness is that he's fictitious. "Hardest shot in hockey, and so fast he can play tennis with himself," says Wolfe. Harry has been threatening to show Keck to his listeners for the past quarter century. "Looks like it's time to bring up Harvey Keck," he will say on the air whenever the Soo Greyhounds are floundering, a pretty regular occurrence in the six years they've been a major

Junior A franchise. When Harry gets into a town, the first question he asks the bus driver is: "Harvey Keck still playing as well as he used to?" Most of them will nod and point to the sign that reads PLEASE DON'T TALK TO THE DRIVER. One, however, recently startled Harry by informing him that Keck had broken his leg and was out for the year.

"The sad thing about all of this," Harry says, "is that night after night it becomes the Wayne Gretzky Show. The team's taken a backseat."

Although the Greyhounds were in the cellar, they trailed fifth-place Sudbury by just a point as they began their recent swing through Ottawa, Peterborough and Hamilton. But they were beaten 9–5, 8–5 and 9–3 on consecutive nights, extending their losing streak to six and making their playoff prospects dimmer. One would never know it to see the press flock into the dressing room after the games.

"It's embarrassing to the other guys," says Angelo Bumbacco, the Soo's general manager, pointing to the crowd of reporters around his star. "We've got to put a stop to this. Let him hold a press conference in another room."

Gretzky is a natural showman. When his favorite number – 9 – was not available this season, he ended up wearing 99. "I tried 14 and 19 at first, but the l's didn't feel quite right on my back," Gretzky says. "The 99 was Muzz' idea."

Muzz, an ex-goalie of no great renown, must have been sensitive to the burden of wearing a 1 on one's back. Born Murray MacPherson, Muzz has been called Muzz so long that he looks like a Muzz. He is a cheerful bowling ball of a man and a practiced referee baiter. Fans battle for seats behind the Greyhound bench to hear him carry on:

"Mike? Mike? Dandy call, Mike. Just tell me one time why that looked like a charge to you when the same play 10 seconds ago didn't. Tell me that, Mike. Mike, I know you're not a homer. Don't look at me like I'm calling you a homer, Mike. You homer! Who said that?"

Muzz' hand, pudgy by nature, is swollen as round as a hockey puck from punching a railing during a recent loss. "Why not give him 99?" he shrugs. "He wanted it. The kid was going to be a marked man anyway. The way he plays, are you kidding?"

To be a marked man in Junior is not a terrific honor. For every player trying to make it into the pros as a goal scorer, there are five or six trying to get there because they can hit people into next week. Then there are the delightful few who don't worry much about next week, concentrating instead on, oh, the next three months in the hospital. Gretzky, so elusive on skates that he is nearly impossible to tag with a hard check, is subject to slashings across the wrists and legs that leave them a mass of welts after each game. Three times this season he has gone to the hospital for postgame X rays.

"It scares me to think there might be some big son of a gun who is just out there on the ice to try to get me out of the game," Gretzky admits. "Guys are always telling me that the next time I touch the puck, they're going to stuff their sticks down my throat. What can you do? You've got to go ahead and tough it and hope they were kidding."

The Greyhounds have loaded their bags onto a chartered, 30-year-old DC-3. Sault Ste. Marie is situated in

Ontario approximately the way El Paso is in Texas, and the Hounds are the only OHA team to travel by plane. Next to Sudbury, which is a 186-mile stone's throw away, Sault Ste. Marie's nearest opponent in the 12-city OHA is 423 miles yonder.

The crew is late, but has carefully remembered to prop open the plane's door in the sub-zero cold. The interior of the DC-3 is lined with the recycled aluminum of old ice chests, and the players huddle in the seats like cubes in a tray. To pass the time, Muzz relates the story of the four-hour roller-coaster flight they took in November of 1975, the day the freighter *Edmund Fitzgerald* sank in a Lake Superior gale. "Thought I was a goner," he says.

"Hey, Boy Wonder," someone yells. "Make some more headlines. Fly us out of here. I'm freezin'!"

Gretzky is used to the flak. He enjoys it, as he enjoys all the attention showered on him. It is a system of checks and balances devised by his teammates so that all the hoopla doesn't go to his head.

Earlier in the year, on a day he was scheduled for a television interview, Gretzky lost an eyebrow and some other, less visible hair to the razors of the Soo veterans. They also loaded his hair with Vaseline. The kid had been initiated. Undaunted, Gretzky had Sylvia Bodner, whose family he lives with in Sault Ste. Marie, apply her eyeliner to his brow and use steam, detergent, lemonade and Bromo – "Kind of made my scalp sore" – to remove the Vaseline in time for the evening news. In another ploy, the team had the Soo police arrest Gretzky for streaking. "I've got to call my agent," he pleaded. He was innocently sitting in the back of the team bus in his shorts and sneakers when the police arrived. And in Ottawa a teammate, masquerading as a press secretary, phoned and asked Gretzky to lunch with Prime Minister Pierre Trudeau. Gretzky took a rain check, explaining that he had to eat a training meal.

"He's got this Boy Wonder thing under control," says Bumbacco, the man who selected Gretzky in the midget draft, even after receiving a letter from Walter Gretzky, an employee of Bell Telephone in Brantford, in which he said he wouldn't let his son play that far from home. "I told Mr. Gretzky we were running a business, and if Wayne was available, we'd take him. Then I had to fly to Brantford and convince him to come."

He did so, but not without the help of Jim and Sylvia Bodner, friends of the Gretzkys from Brantford who had moved to the Soo four years before. "I called up Mr. Gretzky," says Mrs. Bodner, "and it was such a relief to him that Wayne could live with people that he knew. Wayne's father wants so much to be a part of everything that Wayne's going through, and he can't. I know it's hard for him."

For a general manager, Bumbacco is not a dollars-and-cents type. However, as he says, "In dollars and cents, I'd say without Gretzky we'd be averaging 1,100 to 1,200 people per game. With him, we're averaging 2,500."

Bumbacco has been managing one team or another in Sault Ste. Marie for more than 30 years. Seventy of the players who grew up under him have gone on to college on scholarships, and 14 have ended up in professional hockey, among them Chico and Wayne Maki, Lou Nanne, Ivan Boldirev and – the local legends – Tony and Phil Esposito.

"People told me the same thing about Phil that they tell

me about Gretzky: 'He can't skate,'" says Bumbacco. "'Sure,' I tell them, 'You're absolutely right. He can't skate a lick. All he can do is score goals.'"

THE GITCHE GUMEE – LAKE SUPERIOR – IS AN EERIE WHITE wasteland in winter. Freighters like the *Edmund Fitzgerald*, loaded with ore from the Algoma Steel plant, crunch through the channel cut out of the ice in Whitefish Bay. The city of 80,000 is as flat as the frozen waterways around it, and its rows of Monopoly-board houses are broken up only by the billowing smokestacks of the mill and Abitibi Pulp and Paper. It is here that the waters of Lake Superior, boiling into rapids, start their journey to the Atlantic.

Hiawatha was Sault Ste. Marie's first legend, back when the Ojibway nation called that stretch of the river "Pauwating." He wasn't much for hockey, but some of Longfellow's descriptions make Hiawatha sound like something of a cross between Gretzky and Harvey Keck.

Out of childhood into manhood
Now had grown Hiawatha...
Learned in all the lore of old men,
In all youthful sports and pastimes...
He could shoot an arrow from him,
And run forward with such fleetness,
That the arrow fell behind him!

Sam Turco is at the Sault Memorial Gardens the night Gretzky's Greyhounds, as the Sault Ste. Marie team has been dubbed, try to break a seven-game winless streak in a game against Peterborough. He sits in the same seat he has occupied for 30 years, right behind the visitor's bench. Sam came over from Italy in 1912 and worked 25 years at Algoma Steel before he lost his leg to a hangnail that led to gangrene and forced him to start driving a cab.

Sam's got a handshake that Gordie Howe will be hard pressed to match at 72. "Ain't afraid of man nor devil," he says with a quick, hollow rap on his wooden leg. Another night Sam glowers down at Hamilton Coach Bert Templeton. "Cut out that cheap stuff, Bert!" Sam threatens. Rap, rap. "The one hit is fine, but that second shot's cheap stuff!"

A Hamilton forward has just trapped Gretzky against the boards and, surprised to have him pinned, rams the kid's face against the glass for good measure.

"Got to run into him once in a while, Sam," the coach answers with a smile. "Don't get a chance very often."

"That's cheap stuff, Bert, and you know it!" Rap, rap. "I like to give it to Bert. He's all right."

Sam sits back. "See all them little guys?" he says, pointing to the mobs of youngsters in their team jackets. "They only come to see the kid. There wasn't a one here when he was off playing in that Junior tournament in Montreal."

ROSS WINSLADE, HEADMASTER AT SIR JAMES DUNN SCHOOL, which Gretzky and most of the other Greyhound players attend, is also at the game. He has a far better attendance record at the rink than they do at the school. "We've got to be honest with ourselves. They're here to play hockey," he says. "Their education is second. We do what we can." He pauses.

"Gretzky?" he says. "He's an unassuming kid who's doing a helluva job right now just rolling with the punches. I don't worry about his kind of pressure. In a year or so he'll be in my office talking about more money than I'll make the rest of my life.

"The other kids, the fringe players, are the ones with the pressures. They come to a town, settle in a school, then in two months are traded away. They're living out their parents' dreams of glory, maybe, hoping they'll be drafted by the pros – then when they're not, where does that leave them? They're the ones with pressure."

Every year about this time, some of the Greyhounds come into Muzz' office and ask him in what round he thinks they'll be drafted. Most of them won't be picked in any round. "Muzz'll tell them the only draft they'll get is on their butts as they walk out the door," says Tom McLeod, himself a fringe player now in his draft year. "So you try it as a free agent, and if you're not good enough for that, you try the International League."

"And if you're not good enough for that, you go back to Sudbury and be a miner," adds Rich Duguay, who, like McLeod, has been traded twice since the season's opening.

Gretzky is a lucky one. The luckiest of the lucky ones. Right now, the National Hockey League and the World Hockey Association have an agreement with the Junior leagues not to draft any players before they complete their Junior careers at the age of 20. For Gretzky, that will be 1981. But there is very little chance – make that zero chance – he will have to wait that long. His agent, Gus Badali, specializes in procuring six-figure contracts for underage Juniors. Wayne Dillon (now with the New York Rangers), John Tonelli (Houston Aeros) and Mark Napier (Birmingham Bulls) all signed with the WHA while being represented by Badali. And the talent-hungry, publicity-starved WHA will require little arm-twisting to bid for Gretzky. Last September, for instance, Birmingham ignored the established rules of drafting and signed 18-year-old Ken Linseman to a lucrative contract.

The only serious questions are whether the pro leagues will wait until the kid is 18 (Gretzky turned 17 on January 26) and how long and how lucrative his contract will be. Birmingham owner John Bassett, notorious for signing underage Juniors (Linseman, for one), has already waited *nine* years. He was an executive with CFTO television when he saw Gretzky play in a tournament among 8-year-olds.

Gretzky would like to play one more year at the Soo for his $75 a week. "After that, I think I'd be bored," he admits. "Mentally, I'm ready for the pros right now, but physically I'm not."

THE KID IS PUTTING ON A SHOW FOR THE HOME CROWD. HE scores five points as the Greyhounds beat Peterborough 6–3, avenging the previous week's road loss.

Sam Turco hollers with glee and goes into an ice dance, pumping his right elbow and his right knee. "Trouble with hockey today," yells Sam over the noise of the crowd, "is nobody has any fun out there on the ice. Too professional. All these guys want to do is make money. That darn kid has fun, now, don't he?" Rap, rap. "I been here in this seat 30 years, and he stands alone. Yessir. Stands alone. Don't he, Bert! Hee-haw-haw. Don't he!" Rap, rap. "I'm going to have the kid over for a home-cooked dinner some night, and what more can you say about a person than you'd like to have him eat under your own roof. He stands alone, that one."

All the village came and feasted,
All the guests praised Hiawatha,
Called him Strong-Heart, Soan-go-taha!
Called him Loon-Heart, Mahn-go-taysee!

Gretzky would finish his first (and only) season of Junior hockey with 182 points, a rookie record that still stands today.

MINOR MIRACLE UP NORTH

BY JERRY KIRSHENBAUM | DECEMBER 11, 1978

*A 17-year-old Wayne Gretzky couldn't legally drink beer
with his Edmonton Oiler teammates, but the young major
leaguer played with the flair and finesse of an old pro*

(Photograph by Bruce Bennett/Getty Images)

IT HAPPENED A COUPLE OF WEEKS AGO, BUT WAYNE Gretzky still is getting ribbed about it by his Edmonton Oiler teammates. There some of the boys sat, practice over, having a few beers in the bar in the Edmonton Coliseum. And there was Gretzky, enjoying their company and nursing a ginger ale. Then the bartender came over. "Sorry, Wayne," he said, "but you've got to be 18 even to be in here." As his teammates chuckled, Gretzky was politely shown the door.

The laughter was perfectly understandable. After all, Gretzky, the Oilers' 17-year-old rookie center, hadn't ever been stopped like that before. And the way he is performing in the World Hockey Association, who knows when it will happen again.

As a 5-year-old in his native Ontario, Gretzky made a hockey All-Star team otherwise composed of boys 10 and 11. At eight he was showing up 14-year-olds in Bantam League play and being hailed across Canada as the greatest phenom since Bobby Orr. By the time Gretzky was 14, he was living away from home and doing wondrous things against rivals who were 16 and older. Then last year Gretzky, having turned 16, moved to the Junior A level, where the best players are mostly 18 to 20. Playing for the Sault Ste. Marie Greyhounds, the Great Gretzky, as he was now known, scored 70 goals and 112 assists.

After all that, it came as no great surprise when the precocious Gretzky moved into the pros this season, becoming the youngest player in WHA history and the youngest big league performer right now in any team sport. The perennially struggling WHA also boasts the oldest such player, the New England Whalers' 50-year-old Gordie Howe, and Gretzky joined the league with the same sort of ballyhoo that greeted the old man when he arrived with his two sons five years ago.

Seeing Gretzky as somebody who might fill a lot of their empty seats, the foundering Indianapolis Racers signed him to a four-year, $1 million contract, sent him on a whirlwind round of promotional appearances and even organized a Great Gretzky Fan Club. Then last month, just eight games into the season, the financially shaky Racers peddled him to Edmonton, a stronger franchise that, unlike Indianapolis, entertains realistic expectations of getting into the National Hockey League. Peter Pocklington, the Oiler president, said, "We feel that if we're going to be in the NHL, we need a superstar. And Wayne is going to be one."

Gretzky's head could have been spinning over all this, but he is a composed young man. "I was sorry to be leaving the Racers," he says, placating the 1,500 bewildered members of his Indy fan club. Then, pensively stroking some blond facial fuzz that he is careful to shave at least twice a year, he adds, "But the Oilers have shown faith in me, and I'd better produce."

To judge by Gretzky's play so far, there appears little danger of his disappointing anybody. Including three goals scored during his whistlestop in Indianapolis, Gretzky has nine goals in 20 games, and he also has 11 assists. At the same time, his fancy stickhandling and accurate passes have drawn several standing ovations in Edmonton and more oohs and aahs than many players enjoy in an entire career. Still growing at 6 feet and 168 pounds, Gretzky seems to have chicken bones for arms and spindles for legs. But he avoids getting banged around excessively by wriggling and squirting through heavy traffic. Once in the open, he has an effortless, deceptive stride that belies whispers heard in the juniors to the effect that while he had savvy, balance and a lot of other good things, he was not a strong skater.

"That was always the knock on me," Gretzky says. "Well, I feel smoother and faster every day. As I get older, my legs are getting stronger."

When Gretzky joined Edmonton, the team had a 1–4 record. The Oilers are now 12–8 and contending for first place. Glen Sather, the former NHL player who coaches the club, gives Gretzky due credit. "Wayne has innate hockey sense like all the great players," says Sather, who played for Boston in 1966 when Orr was a rookie with the Bruins. "Coming out of his end, he always seems in position to take the pass. And when he gets the puck he knows where everybody is, the way a center is supposed to. I hate to put this on him, but a player like Gretzky comes along only once every 10 years. He's not up there with Orr, Hull and Howe yet, but he's not far away, either."

————

THAT GRETZKY IS ALREADY PLAYING PRO HOCKEY DOES
not sit well with Canadian amateur officials, who had
been assured by both the NHL and WHA that juniors
under 20 would not be signed to pro contracts. But those
pledges were made by league offices, not by teams. While
NHL clubs have abided by the gentlemen's agreement,
WHA teams, buoyed by court rulings, have been signing
underage players at will. And when Nelson Skalbania,
the majority owner of the Racers, made his million-dollar
offer last summer, Gretzky leaped at it. He eventually
signed a personal services contract with Skalbania while
they were flying somewhere over Alberta in Skalbania's
private jet.

"I've got one semester of high school to go, and the
only reason I could think of to stay in the juniors was to
graduate," Gretzky says. "But an offer like that is hard to
turn down."

Gretzky hoped to get his diploma while playing with
the Racers and, in fact, enrolled in two courses in the adult
division of Indianapolis' Broad Ripple High School. His
teammates, who nicknamed him Brinks because of his big
contract, took a liking to him, as did the members of the
Great Gretzky Fan Club. However, after an encouraging
turnout of 11,728 for the Racers' opening game – a 6–3 loss
to Winnipeg in which Gretzky went scoreless – attendance
dropped to the 5,000-to-7,000 level.

That settled matters for Skalbania, a Vancouver entrepre-
neur who formerly owned the Edmonton team. He sold
Gretzky, Winger Peter Driscoll and Goalie Eddie Mio to his
old club for $850,000. Having paid Gretzky just $60,000 so
far, and since Driscoll and Mio were essentially throw-ins,

Skalbania reaped a windfall; he insisted, though, that the sale was his only hope of keeping the Racers afloat.

Might it be that Skalbania had actually planned to unload Gretzky for a fast profit all along? Suspecting as much, some irate season ticket holders in Indianapolis reacted to the sale by filing a class-action suit, and the Indianapolis *Star* taunted the club's absentee owner with the headline HEY NELSON, GO BACK TO SKALBANIA. Meanwhile, the last-place Racers are 4–15–2 and apparently trying to hang on until such time as the NHL might absorb choice WHA franchises like the Oilers, at which point less choice franchises such as their own would be indemnified for consenting to pack it in.

Despite his diplomatically correct expressions of regret over leaving Indianapolis, Gretzky knows that the future is brighter in Edmonton. The NHL is interested in oil-rich Edmonton because it is a good hockey town, with a new 15,248-seat arena. The NHL also could use another western franchise or two for geographical balance. The Oilers led the WHA last season with an average attendance of 10,222, and while this year's figure is running about the same, team officials expect Gretzky's presence to send it upward as soon as the people in Edmonton stop celebrating their Eskimos' victory over Montreal in the Grey Cup two weeks ago.

In the meantime, Gretzky has made himself at home. On arriving from Indy he entered the Oiler locker room, took one look at the strapping form of Dave Semenko, a 6'3" left wing nicknamed "Cement," and cracked, "I want this guy on my line so I can look after him." Gretzky cavorts around the ice at practices with a smile on his face and actually sings along when *O Canada* is played before games.

But Gretzky realizes that his youth sets him apart from other pro players. He will be able to drink with the boys when he turns 18 on January 26, but the fact remains that the next-youngest Oiler, rookie Wing Dave Hunter, is nearly three years his elder, and that other teammates are old enough to be his father. Last week Pocklington ran Oiler players and their wives through a three-day "positive thinking" course for executives that dealt with subjects such as child rearing and family finances. When the final all-day session ended, Gretzky wearily admitted, "I wondered what I was doing there."

With his parents 2,100 miles away in Brantford, Ont., Gretzky is boarding with a family in Edmonton. Except for a 1979 Thunderbird, he has few extravagances and, rather than squander his newfound riches, submits to an allowance so stringent that teammates applauded the other day when he decided to buy a plastic scraper for cleaning ice off his windshield. Gretzky hopes to enroll in high school next month and – finally – graduate. And, he says, he means to pal around with people his own age. Of course, that didn't prevent him from taking an older woman of 18 out for dinner the other night, his first date in Edmonton.

"When I'm 23 I don't want to look back and feel I missed being a teen-ager," Gretzky says. "I want to be a hockey player and a normal 17-year-old. People say, 'Aren't you missing something playing hockey?' The way I look at it, I'm not missing *anything*. I'm getting extra."

Gretzky's level-headedness is matched by his faith in his abilities. "He's confident as hell," says Sather. "He firmly believes he's going to be the best player in the world." To gauge his frustration during the Oilers' 8–2 rout last week of Gretzky's former Indianapolis mates in the Coliseum, it can't happen fast enough to suit him. He played well and picked up an assist on a goal by Wing Bill Flett, but couldn't buy a goal himself despite several good chances. One was a breakaway on which he was stopped by Racer Goalie Gary Inness. On the bench, Sather said, "You'll get the next one."

The following day Gretzky was still brooding about the missed breakaway. "In the juniors the goalie wouldn't have stopped that shot," he said, shaking his head. "The goaltending is better in the pros – that's the big difference." He brightened. "Otherwise, there isn't as much slashing and highsticking as there was in the juniors, and they let you play hockey more. I'm actually getting more opportunities than I ever did. In that way, playing here hasn't been that much of an adjustment." He was smiling now. "In fact, it's been pretty easy."

So far, that seems to be the story of the Great Gretzky's life.

Gretzky scored a remarkable 110 points in his WHA rookie season. When the Oilers were one of the four WHA teams to merge with the NHL after the 1978–79 season, he silenced critics who wondered if his game would work in the NHL by putting up 137 points as an NHL rookie.

THE BEST AND GETTING BETTER

BY E.M. SWIFT | OCTOBER 12, 1981

At 20, Wayne Gretzky was, without question,
the NHL's top player. All that was left to ask was:
How good would he become?

(Photograph by Paul Kennedy)

WAYNE GRETZKY SHARES A 14TH-FLOOR TWO-BEDROOM condominium in Edmonton, Alberta with Kevin Lowe, a teammate on the Edmonton Oilers. Lowe has temporarily moved out so Gretzky's mother, Phyllis, and his 18-year-old sister, Kim, who are visiting from Brantford, Ont., can stay with Wayne during the first week of the Canada Cup series. The night before, Team Canada, for whom Gretzky plays, won its first game, beating Finland 9–0. Today the team practiced at noon, and it has the afternoon off. Phyllis is sitting at one end of the living room couch, and Kim is sprawled at the other end, looking slightly catatonic. Gus Badali, Gretzky's agent and a friend of the family's, is seated across the room beside a stack of life-sized cardboard cutouts of the Boy Wonder himself modeling jeans, which are headed for clothing stores around Canada. A man from GWG jeans, the brand Gretzky endorses, sits near Badali. Gretzky is seated at his desk opening mail, and his girl friend, 19-year-old Vickie Moss, is bouncing off the walls, as usual. She's what's known as vivacious. It's a pretty good crowd for a weekday afternoon, but Gretzky is used to that. He likes gatherings. "I'm not big on independency," he says.

"So who wants to hear my song?" asks Vickie.

Everyone would like to, but no one is feeling chipper enough to make much of a fuss over the offer. Gretzky had a midnight curfew the night before, but his guests were all out on the town till four a.m. Drinking ice water seems to be their top priority. Badali finally gurgles, "I do." Phyllis and Kim are content just to rattle their ice cubes in concurrence.

This will never do. "Who wants to hear my song?" Vickie, a budding vocalist, demands. She's a very pretty girl, but she's also an accomplished arm wrestler, and this time there are five or six *I do's* and half as many *please's*. Vickie flashes an accommodating smile and turns on the tape, a fight song for the Edmonton Drillers soccer team that she recently recorded.

"Chalk up one more win for the Drillers," the song begins. Other lyrics encourage the Drillers goalward, and Vickie is singing along with herself, pretending to kick and block shots at the appropriate moments. It's a terrific little number, and if it's possible for a career to be launched by a soccer fight song, hers will be. When it's over she asks, "Want to hear it again?" and she's virtually bowled over with *I do's* and *please's* and the clicking of cubes.

Alan Thicke calls from Los Angeles. There isn't much news to be had there about the Canada Cup, and he wants to hear about the games. Thicke is sort of a Canadian Merv Griffin, and Wayne and Vickie were guests on his show this summer. Gretzky calls everyone older than he "Mister," and when he says "Mr. Thicke" over the phone, he makes Alan sound like a frozen milk shake. They talk hockey for a while. Then Mr. Thicke tells Gretzky about a funny thing that happened. Anne Murray, the singer, who's also Canadian, had called him that morning to find out if he had any amusing stories she could use for an upcoming concert. Mr. Thicke said he did. He tells Gretzky one. It must be a pretty good one because Gretzky is really tickled when he hangs up, and can't wait to relay it.

Problem is, Gretzky is a bad storyteller. He laughs all the way through his delivery, so when he gets to the punch line, it doesn't sound like a punch line. However, that doesn't keep him from trying. He's a game one and outgoing when relaxed. He has been like that ever since he was a kid – always ready with an answer, always striving to be the center of attention. This story has something to do with a supposed rumor that Murray wants to go out with Gretzky because she would like to find out what the "Great" stands for. That's what the GWG jeans people call him – The Great Wayne Gretzky. In the newspaper headlines it's usually THE GREAT GRETZKY. It has been like that since he was 16 years old. Now, at 20, he carries the title well.

It wasn't that the joke was so funny to Gretzky. It was the idea that Murray, the singer, and Thicke, the talk-show host, would casually refer to him in such a way – ho-hum, just another celebrity-rumor joke. Hockey players aren't used to that. Not since Bobby Orr came into the NHL in 1966 as an 18-year-old has anyone captured the imagination of hockey fans the way Gretzky has, and no one has appealed to the general public like Gretzky since Bobby Hull appeared on the cover of TIME in 1968. Gretzky, a center, is the most dangerous offensive player in the game, the most exciting, the most fun to watch. But he's more than that. He's The Kid. There has always been something special about that sobriquet, something that reaches out to everyone. The Kid. Someone who will grow up before our eyes.

"He's only 20, and he's torn the league apart two years in a row," says Red Berenson, coach of the St. Louis Blues. "It's scary to think what he might do before he's done."

Scary to Berenson, who must coach against Gretzky, but fun for the rest of us because we know, as good as he is now, that we haven't seen his best. There came a time with Orr, who's generally acknowledged to be the greatest hockey player of all time, when we knew "that's it, he can't show us any more, no one can." The remaining question was, how long could he continue to play at such an extraordinary level? But with Gretzky, we still don't know what his best will be. We can't yet know just how many points this phenomenal performer will amass in a single season once he matures physically and his team matures around him. The Oilers are a young club. They have no other star. "The mystery about Gretzky is the things he has been able to do with the players he has had around him," says Bill Torrey, general manager of the New York Islanders. "Everything that happens when he's on the ice revolves around him. Either he's got the puck or the other team does."

What Gretzky did last year, his second in the NHL, was break Phil Esposito's single-season scoring record (152 points) and Orr's assist mark (102). Both had been set 10 years ago and had never been seriously threatened. Gretzky was 19 at the start of last season, 5'11" and 165 pounds. He either scored or assisted on a staggering 50% of Edmonton's goals (when Esposito set his record, he was in on 38% of

Boston's league-record 399 goals), finishing with 55 goals and 109 assists for 164 points. He became the first NHL player since 1917–18 to average more than two points a game, and he won his second Most Valuable Player award.

He had the type of year no one had thought possible, but most hockey experts now assume Gretzky will surpass it. No other star has ever had his best year when he was 19. Orr had his best at 22; Esposito at 28; Hull at 29. Why should Gretzky be any different? What might happen if he gets to play alongside another exceptional player, the way Esposito did with Orr? Edmonton has some of the best young players in the game, and one day they may be superb. What then? Will The Kid then stop being The Kid? Will we finally sit back and say, "So that's how good he really is" and start to worry about how long we will have him?

Gretzky played Junior A hockey four years ago with a mediocre team called the Sault Ste. Marie Greyhounds. He already was a media sensation, a 16-year-old dazzling a league of 20-year-olds. He was polite, well-spoken and charming – rare traits in the hockey world – and the public and press ate him up. Kids identified with him because he was scrawny and not very fast. Yet he would go out there and stickhandle through all these hulking goons, fulfilling the fantasies of every boy who has ever picked up a hockey stick. It wasn't as if he had an incredible body like Hull's, or amazing grace like Orr's; Gretzky just kind of slithered by you or threaded a pass between your skates. But a lot of scouts had misgivings about him because 158-pound hockey players, which was what Gretzky weighed then, weren't in vogue. Slow 158-pound hockey players, especially.

Gretzky was never actually slow. He just looked it. "He

never had to skate well," says his father, Walter, "because as a kid he could stay in the same place and beat a player three or four times." Walter, not surprisingly, is responsible for Wayne's remarkable early development. He had his son on the backyard rink before Wayne was three years old. He began teaching him fundamentals when Wayne was four. At six Wayne began playing in a league with 10-year-olds. The backyard rink wasn't just for yuks. Walter set up pylons and had Wayne practice crossovers and figure eights. He would throw a puck into the corner and tell Wayne to get it. After Wayne had chased several pucks around the boards, Walter would say, "Watch me." He'd throw it in again and skate to a spot where he could intercept the puck as it caromed around the boards. "I always told him, 'Skate to where the puck's going to be, not to where it has been,'" says Walter. "I've never believed that it's an instinctive thing that one kid anticipates better than another."

Gretzky's anticipation, whether innate or learned, has long been astounding; he always seemed to know what his opponent would do with the puck. And he knew exactly where everyone was on the ice. Ask him where his four teammates were on a given goal, and he could tell you. He also could tell you what they *should* have been doing if they were out of position. He and his father would watch hockey games together, and as they drove home, Walter, who never advanced beyond Junior B hockey, would ask Wayne if he remembered such-and-such a play. Then they would talk about the options each skater had. Most coaches will tell you the most important trait a player can have is speed. Walter disagrees. "He has got to be aware of where everybody is all the time," Walter says. "His mind has to be like a camera. That's going to make his reaction time that much quicker."

It's true. Gretzky always looks as if he has been given a head start when there's a race toward a loose puck. His anticipation makes him faster than he appears to be. Says Lou Nanne, general manager of the Minnesota North Stars, "Gretzky has to see the game five times slower than the average guy."

As a youngster Gretzky saw *life* five times slower than the average guy. He looked ahead. When Wayne was 16, nice-looking, famous and blessed with an imminently marketable talent, he could have gone out with just about any girl in Ontario. But he seldom even went on a date and never saw anyone special. He didn't drink, drive or smoke – not because he didn't want to but because there would be time for all that later.

"My father always told me to get what I wanted most and the rest [girls, cars, money, fame] would follow," he says. Gretzky was living on the straight and narrow; he knew exactly what he wanted and the quickest way to get it. Never mind what he was telling the press: that he was considering going to university instead of pursuing a hockey career. "Gretzky hesitates about a pro career for the finest of reasons – education," one story in the Toronto Star read. It was such obvious tripe; he already had Badali as an agent, for heaven's sake. You see, Gretzky had been in the public eye since he was eight, and he had learned to manipulate his image through the press.

Gretzky turned pro at 17, signing a four-year contract worth $875,000 with the Indianapolis Racers of the WHA. It was crazy, everyone thought, asking a 161-pound

17-year-old – Boy Wonder or not – to play in the pros. Lunacy.

Gretzky played eight games with the Racers before the club's financial troubles forced owner Nelson Skalbania to sell Gretzky's contract to Peter Pocklington, owner of the Oilers, for $850,000. Pocklington renegotiated Gretzky's contract, tying him up for nine years, with two six-year options – 21 years in all. The agreement guarantees Gretzky somewhere around $300,000 a year.

Now that deal looks like a steal. "I didn't know I was going to get more than 50 goals each of my first two years in the NHL," says Gretzky. He's trying to renegotiate, though he isn't yet pushing the matter that hard. Glen Sather, the coach and general manager of the Oilers, points out that the Oilers took a risk in signing such a young player to a contract of such long duration. He recalls an incident in Gretzky's first pro season that convinced him The Kid was for real, that Gretzky had been worth the risk. It occurred in a game against the Cincinnati Stingers, when a defensive lapse by Gretzky cost Edmonton a goal. Sather benched him for more than a period and then, with the Oilers trailing 2–1, played him again in the third period. "He could have pouted and sulked," says Sather, "but when I put him back in, he scored a hat trick and we won 5–2. That to me was the turning point of his pro career. Not just anyone could keep his motivation with a contract like his. But he wants to be the best."

Gretzky finished the season with 110 points and was named WHA Rookie of the Year. Equally significant, he didn't miss a game. He had proved he could handle the faster pace and bigger players of the pro game. Still, when the NHL and WHA merged before the 1979–80 season, few observers believed Gretzky could duplicate his scoring totals in the NHL. The NHL had little respect for the upstart WHA, and it wasn't about to give some 18-year-old kid from an inferior league the benefit of the doubt. "Everybody said, 'He's scrawny; he'll never tear up this league the way he did the WHA,'" recalls Torrey. That was all Gretzky needed to hear.

Gretzky set a goal for himself: getting at least as many points in his first year in the NHL as he had in his WHA season. If he didn't, the NHL, the media and the public all would probably slight his accomplishments in the other league. Gretzky never doubted for a moment that he could achieve his goal, but even he was surprised at the kind of year he had in 1979–80. He tied for the league scoring championship with 137 points, won the Lady Byng Memorial Trophy as the NHL's most gentlemanly player and was named the league's MVP. Pocklington rewarded those efforts with a Ferrari. Gretzky's father had been right. The rest would follow.

Curiously, despite Gretzky's brilliant debut, most teams continued to defend against him last season as though he were simply another player. "I honestly believe there were still people around who thought of Wayne as a flash in the pan," says Sather. The result was Gretzky's record-shattering 164 points. The Kid was for real, all right.

But it was Gretzky's performance in the playoffs that convinced everyone he was more than just a scorer, that he was one of those rare players who can lift a team onto his shoulders and carry it upward. The Oilers finished the regular season in 14th place, with a 29–35–16 record. Their first-round playoff opponent was Montreal, which finished third and came into postseason play with a 24–1–2 record in its last 27 home games. The Canadiens were healthy, and Guy Lafleur, Montreal's leader, was eager to have an excellent series against Gretzky to atone for what had been for him a dismal season. The Canadiens' goalie, Richard Sevigny, went so far as to predict that Lafleur would put Gretzky "in his back pocket." That remark was a grievous error.

Gretzky reads everything written about him. I remember, in Sault Ste. Marie, when I was there writing about the 16-year-old Gretzky, a local reporter asked me what I thought of Gretzky's play. I said something to the effect that offensively he was peerless but defensively he had a long way to go. No one cared much about defense in junior hockey. The next game, Gretzky was the principal star, with a goal and a couple of assists in a 4–2 win. Afterward, as he walked by me, he asked slyly, "Good enough defense for you?" He had been flawless in his own end all night, and he was just proud enough to let me know it, in case I'd been too stupid to notice.

Edmonton beat Montreal 6–3 in the first game of the playoffs, and Gretzky tied a Stanley Cup record by getting five assists. And just in case Sevigny had been too stupid to notice, after the Oilers' sixth goal Gretzky skated by the Canadien net and patted the general vicinity of his back pocket. No question about it. The Kid has got brass.

When Edmonton won the second game 3–1, the Montreal fans rose to applaud the Oilers as they celebrated their victory at center ice. It was as if the fans had sensed the baton being passed from Lafleur, who had been the most exciting player in hockey the six previous years, to Gretzky. It was kind of a sad thing, but it was too obvious to ignore. Right there in the Montreal Forum, *in the playoffs*, Gretzky was dominant, playing on a different level from even Lafleur. When the papers tried to depict the series as a matter of Gretzky-over-Lafleur, Gretzky rose to his rival's defense, saying, "One guy can't win the Stanley Cup, or the Boston Bruins would have won it seven straight years with Orr. The better the team plays, the better you play." It works the other way around, too, but only with some players, the great ones. That's what was happening in this series. The Oilers won the next game 6–2 to complete the sweep. Lafleur had one point in the three games. When Gretzky was on the ice and the teams were at even strength, Edmonton outscored Montreal 11–0.

In the next round the Oilers lost to the defending Stanley Cup champion Islanders four games to two, but not before Gretzky had made his way into one of Torrey's poems to Nanne.

> *This epistle will be rather short and sweet*
> *I need time to figure a way to keep number 99 off the*
>   *score sheet.*
> *It's scary to think disaster lurks due to some 20-year-old,*
> *But after looking at the tapes, Gretzky is something to*
>   *behold.*

The Islanders' strategy was to hit Gretzky every opportunity they got, which is easier said than done. "He's an open pond guy," says Torrey, "an eel who's hard to hit because he's not around the boards much. But Dave Langevin caught him with a helluva check, and Bryan Trottier hit him once. Those shots slowed him down. By the fifth and sixth games, Gretzky wasn't the same player he was in the first three or four."

Sather noticed it, too. "They bumped him a lot more in the last few games," he says. "He was tired against the Islanders. He won't ever admit that to you. But then again, you can't rest him if he's the only guy winning games for you."

Nevertheless, the series was a lot closer than New York had dreamed it would be, and it served notice that the Oilers may be the team of the not-too-distant future. Edmonton, needless to say, is rather pleased to have Gretzky aboard. For one thing, he fits the city's image – young, vibrant, confident. Edmontonians are ready to take on the world. The balance of power in Canada has rapidly been shifting west, where the money is, so it's only fitting that the present and future star of the national sport should come from this boomtown.

"They should rename the place Gretmonton," says Al Morganti of *The Philadelphia Inquirer*. Gretzky's picture is everywhere – on jigsaw puzzles, T shirts, key chains, billboards, television, drugstore counters. About every third kid wears a number 99 jersey to the hockey games. Gretzky endorses seven products, ranging from hockey sticks to chocolate bars. His best-known advertisement in the States is an engaging 7Up commercial he does with his 14-year-old brother, Keith. The income from these activities nearly matches what Gretzky makes playing hockey. The Kid is hot.

This fact has not escaped the attention of the brighter executives around the NHL, who have winced at the league's pathetic attempts to market itself in the U.S. Nanne thinks that the NHL should start a films division, with the first assignment being to produce a highlight movie of

Gretzky. Then The Kid could show up on, say, *The Tonight Show*, and television viewers could see the impossible things he does on the ice. You can't do them justice by talking about them. Eddie Mio, an Edmonton goaltender, says that even the players can't fully appreciate what Gretzky does because they're watching from ice level. "I sat in the stands one game when I was injured, and it was magic," says Mio.

Magic sells. Sather thinks the league should come right out and make a commercial about The Kid and pay for it to be aired. "You've got to create some sort of hero image in the U.S." he says. Gordie Howe, who once filled that role, has said, "The NHL needs someone to hang its hat on, and Gretzky looks like a hat tree."

He's already the most recognized athlete in Canada. Gretzky made at least two appearances in each of Canada's eight largest cities over the summer, and once, in Montreal, 7,500 people came to see him in a shopping center. During an autograph-signing session at a Toronto food fair, two girls stood and watched him for four hours, never saying a word, apparently too love-sick to do anything but gawk. "It wasn't normal," says Badali. Gretzky finally asked that the girls be requested to move along – they were giving him the willies – and he undoubtedly lost two fans as a result.

Badali, who handles Gretzky's schedule, is a gentle, soft-spoken man, and for years he has told Gretzky to model himself after Howe. He certainly could do worse. Howe, always modest, always patient with strangers, is beloved in Canada. Gretzky is following the same pattern and gaining similar affection. "So far he has been willing to take advice," says Badali. "As long as he does that, things will be all right."

It can be trying, though. Gretzky has been on the straight

and narrow for a long time now. So much of growing up is learning from your mistakes, and it seems as if Gretzky hasn't been allowed to make any for years. "Back in the Sault Ste. Marie days, I did what I wanted to do," he says. "Right now my life isn't in my hands as far as summertime goes. It's in my management's hands."

In addition to trips around Canada, Gretzky made three appearances in New York City this summer and one in Las Vegas. Leroy Neiman painted a portrait of him, the original of which is immodestly priced at $125,000. Prints can be purchased for $2,675 in the U.S., $3,200 in Canada. Gretzky also taped a segment for ABC's *Kids Are People Too*, which is filmed in New York. As a surprise, the producers flew in his three brothers: Keith, Glen, 12, and Brent, 9. Gretzky was surprised, all right, but when his brothers ran out onto the stage, he hardly changed expression. "Nothing surprises me anymore," he says. After the show, Gretzky, alone with all his brothers for one of the few times in his life, took them to a Mets game.

Gretzky is discreetly affectionate with people to whom he feels close. A family friend once described him as "a toucher." Vickie, who describes Gretzky and herself as having a "great, close, backing-each-other, busy relationship," says, "Probably what's most important to him is pleasing his father. His father's brilliant. He's always right. And he's old-fashioned when it comes to family upbringing. When he says 'Jump,' they say, 'How high?' They all have a lot of discipline. It's in their blood."

Even with mere acquaintances, Gretzky displays a puppy-like desire to please, to be liked. For a while he winked at everyone. "He's more outgoing and seemingly younger than Orr was at the same age," says Nanne. "As a result, Gretzky's presence does not command that mystique. He's more like a kid brother or a son."

Orr wasn't particularly concerned about cultivating his image. He was very much a player's player. One of the guys. Gretzky is well liked by his teammates, but he's clearly on a different track. In 15 years it's unlikely that he'll be a scout or a general manager or a player representative. He'll be a corporate executive or a movie star, or something outside hockey. He mingles better with people outside his profession than those in it. The thought of Thicke and Murray discussing him so tickled Gretzky because he has not fully come to grips with the breadth of his celebrity. "He still thinks of himself as an average Canadian guy," says Sather, "and the public responds to that."

This summer in Las Vegas, Gretzky practically gawked when he met Judy Landers of *B.J. and the Bear*. Says Mio, who was there, too, and admits he did the same, "It's all right for me to do that but Gretzky shouldn't. He's one of *them*."

Gretzky took August off from personal appearances to get in shape for the Canada Cup. Not that he ever gets really out of shape. He ran a little and lifted weights, beefing up to 173 pounds. In strength tests the Oilers held in 1979, Gretzky finished last. Yet on tests that measured endurance and recuperative powers, his performance was outstanding. Those results help explain why he picks up so many of his points at the tail end of shifts or in the third period. Since turning pro, Gretzky's speed has improved greatly, and he's now one of the fastest forwards in the league, despite an awkward skating style. "He's not what you'd call fluid," his father says. "It's because of his arms. Watch his arms. I always told him to hold them away from his body. You can't do anything with your elbows tucked up against your body, but keeping them out makes you look funny when you skate."

When the best players in the NHL assembled for Team Canada, the coach, Scotty Bowman of the Buffalo Sabres, assigned Gretzky to center a line that had Lafleur as right wing. Bowman later settled on Gil Perreault, who is naturally a center, as their left wing. "They couldn't wait to play with Gretzky," Bowman says. Lafleur and Perreault each had had his most disappointing season in 1980–81, but in Team Canada workouts each was skating as he had in his prime. "The Kid has gone into rejuvenating careers," said Frank Orr of the *Toronto Star*. It became obvious how badly Lafleur missed his old centerman, Jacques Lemaire, who left the Canadiens after the 1978–79 season. Since then no one has been able to get the puck to him consistently. With Gretzky, it was as if he and Lafleur had played together forever. "Lafleur is kind of a free-spirit player, as is Gretzky," says Berenson, who was one of Bowman's assistants on Team Canada. "They can anticipate each other's moves. And they have a mutual respect, the kind great, great players have for each other."

They played with total selflessness. No egos were at stake, no attempts at one-upmanship were made. At times, they over-passed, forgoing good shots in an effort to make the perfect play. Perreault caught the spirit, too, and until he broke his leg, they were the best line in the tournament. In the world. But it was Gretzky's show. He had brought out the best in the other stars. Gretzky, though, doesn't accept that assessment.

"He doesn't think of himself as the greatest, because of his respect for Guy," says Mio, who, of Gretzky's peers, may know him best. "He just loves Guy. He'd like to have the same public image as Lafleur – not sophisticated and not a jerk."

Gretzky isn't the only one who loves Lafleur. During the Canada Cup games in Edmonton, the fans chanted "Guy! Guy! Guy!" whenever he touched the puck. It was the first time he had been the object of such an outpouring of affection, and Lafleur joked that it was Edmonton's way of thanking him for the way he played in last spring's playoffs. But it was more than that; it was for services rendered, for the years when he was the greatest and carried the burden that will be Gretzky's for the next little while. "They give more to the game," Sather says of the few true superstars. "They care about it more. Gretzky's got to pay his dues yet, but I'm 100% sure he'll do it. The way it shows is how the team around him plays better each year."

Sather thinks this season will be Gretzky's toughest. The main reason is that with the new unbalanced schedule Edmonton will play each of the clubs in its division eight times. "They're going to have to figure out a way to stop him," Sather says. "Last year you'd play a team once and might not see it again for two months."

Theories abound on how to stop Gretzky. The Bruins enjoyed some success by assigning a man to shadow him all night. Berenson, though, doesn't believe that tactic makes good sense. "If Gretzky plays 40 minutes," he says, "and I play my best defensive player 40 minutes, sooner or later Gretzky's going to score because he's better at his game than my guy is at his. Furthermore, Edmonton's going to win because when Gretzky's out there, he always has a chance to score, and my defensive line has very little chance of doing so. You have to stick with what you do best." It should be noted, however, that Gretzky got five goals and two assists in *one* game against St. Louis last season while the Blues presumably were concentrating on what they do best.

Nanne has a different idea. "It sounds stupid," he says, "but the way to play him is to put as many guys on him as it takes to keep him away from the puck and leave his teammates alone and hope they don't score. You can't say that if you cover Gretzky's linemates he'll have no one to pass to, because he creates his own scoring opportunities."

Another Nanne idea is to push the goal back against the boards so that Gretzky can't set up behind it. When Gretzky was 14, his junior coach told him to find a place for himself in the offensive zone where he wouldn't always get knocked down. So he went behind the net, and the tactic may revolutionize the game. "It's like having an extra player out there, particularly on the power play," says Cliff Fletcher, general manager of the Calgary Flames. "He uses the net like a pick."

A puck fired around the boards invariably passes behind the goal – remember the drills Gretzky's father put him through – so when Gretzky is back there, he's easy to hit with a pass. The defenseman then has a problem. If he chases Gretzky from one side of the net, Gretzky will scoot out the other. If two players come after him, one from either side, Gretzky will slide the puck to one of the areas they've just vacated. A teammate should be sweeping in. And if the other team leaves him alone back there, he either will thread a pass onto someone's stick in front or come out in front himself, forcing a defender to commit himself. "The best you can hope for is to get on him quickly and force him to his backhand," says Berenson without much enthusiasm, because Gretzky, of course, will find a solution to that, too.

TEAM CANADA IS PRACTICING IN EDMONTON. THE STYLE OF play in the NHL is starting to change, starting to adopt aspects of the European game, which emphasizes speed and passing over size and power. Gretzky is now a role model, and it's possible that other young Canadian forwards will begin setting up behind the net, flicking accurate passes to teammates, using brains instead of brawn. In the post-Orr years, every young defenseman in Canada carried the puck into the offensive zone, an unfortunate habit that probably set back hockey in North America 10 years. But this style of Gretzky's, it will be something else, if it catches on. It's fun, creating plays. It can be seen in the way Lafleur, Perreault and Gretzky practice this day, in the way they weave and pass, nearly laughing.

Two girls are watching. They're oblivious to the wonderful hockey they are seeing. One says, "Did you hear?"

"What?"

"Wayne and Vickie are breaking up."

(*Hopefully*) "Really?"

"For sure. I feel really bad for her. She was the most popular girl in school, you know."

(*Even more hopefully*) "Are you sure?"

"Poz."

(*Sighs*) "I'd like to meet him. Maybe I could find out exactly why they call him [*giggles*] The Great Wayne Gretzky."

The Canada Cup games will now shift to Winnipeg, and a bus will take the players to the airport. Everyone is aboard but Gretzky. The Kid is late again. As the team waits, Phyllis Gretzky sends someone onto the bus to get Lafleur to sign a picture of him and her son. Lafleur is one of Phyllis' favorite players.

Gretzky arrives with Vickie, embarrassed to have caused the delay. His sister and Badali have gone to get Gretzky's suitcase. He and Vickie haven't broken up, but as long as schoolgirls carry hope in their hearts, there will be rumors.

"Bet you $5 The Kid kisses her good-by," someone on the bus says. The players start an "Ohhhhhhhh" that builds and builds, like before the opening kickoff at a college football game.

"Ohhhhhhhh...." This is going to be really funny. "Ohhhhhhhhhh...." Gretzky does nothing, and they run out of air. Then Badali arrives with the suitcase, and Gretzky gives Vickie an affectionate kiss on the cheek. Everyone on the bus boos. You see, The Kid has timing. Why do you think they call him Great?

Gretzky put up points at a phenomenal pace in the 1981–82 season, rewriting the record book en route to proving himself the greatest player of all time.

THE LORD OF THE RINKS

BY MIKE DELNAGRO | FEBRUARY 15, 1982

As Wayne Gretzky strengthened his claim to being the NHL's top star, his Oilers kept on winning, getting ever closer to their goal – the Stanley Cup

(Photograph by Arthur Schatz/Time & Life Pictures/Getty Images)

THE COACH IS STEAMING. THE BUS HE'S RIDING IN IS crowded and hot. Clenched in his fist is a piece of paper – a roster of the Edmonton Oilers. The coach's own team, an established NHL power, has just been outskated, outhit and – what really tees him off – outscored by the miserable list of names he holds. Pen in hand, he flattens the piece of paper and circles the name Wayne Gretzky. Again. And again. Now he puts slash marks through Wayne Gretzky. Now he inks out Wayne Gretzky, every last trace, down to the serif on the final y. He indicates the great blot of ink. "This way, 75% of Edmonton is gone," he says. "No way they beat us." He pauses, deep in thought, and then adds, "But no one around can blot out Wayne Gretzky."

Or the Gretzky-led Oilers. They are the slickest, quickest, most explosive club in the NHL, a boom team from a boomtown. With wins last weekend over the Maple Leafs (5–1) and the Rangers (8–4), the Oilers ran their record to 35–13–10 and strengthened their grip on first place, not only in the Smythe Division but also in the whole 21-team league. At this time last season only one team had a worse record than Edmonton's. What's going on here?

For one thing, in the 21-year-old Gretzky, the Oilers have

far and away the most dominant player in the game. He's re-rewriting the NHL record book so completely that last week league headquarters in Montreal felt obliged to issue a press release detailing his accomplishments to date. Seven pages. In brief, it said that Gretzky is having the finest season any NHL player has ever had.

Now in his third year in the league, Gretzky probably will break all the major NHL single-season scoring records. In 1980–81 he broke Phil Esposito's scoring mark of 152 points by getting 164 and Bobby Orr's assist record of 102, with 109. This year, as of last Sunday, Gretzky had 69 goals and 83 assists for 152 points. And with 25% of the season to go, he should topple both records again. He'll also surpass Esposito's hallowed mark of 76 goals in a season. "He's made the record book obsolete," says North Star General Manager Lou Nanne. "From now on, Gretzky's only point of reference is himself."

The Oilers actually began to surge near the close of last season. They lost just four of their final 20 games on the regular schedule. Then in the playoffs, they upset Montreal in three straight and won two games from the Islanders before going under. At the time Gretzky was 20 years old. So were high-scoring wings Mark Messier, Glenn Anderson and Jari Kurri. Edmonton's top two defensemen, Kevin Lowe and Paul Coffey, were 21 and 19, respectively. "We went through bad times together, grew up together, lost together," says Gretzky. "Now's our turn to win together."

Much of the credit for Edmonton's success belongs to Glen Sather, 37, the Oilers' coach, G.M. and president. After bouncing among six NHL teams in nine seasons as a wild-eyed utility forward, Sather closed out his playing career in the now-defunct WHA with Edmonton in 1975–76. Bep Guidolin, then the Oiler coach, took a shine to Sather and had him run a few practices. One day late that season, Guidolin called Sather into his office and said, "Tonight I want you either in the stands or behind the bench." Guidolin was fired shortly thereafter, and Sather has been in charge of the Oilers ever since.

In 1979, when Edmonton joined the NHL, Sather committed the Oilers to building through the draft. He wanted speed and youth, not grinding veterans. His phone rang constantly. Often it was Scotty Bowman of the Sabres, Bill Torrey of the Islanders or Keith Allen of the Flyers. "Wolves howling at the door," says Sather. His players were unproved talents, and it would have been easy to trade any one of them for three or four solid veterans. In January of 1981 Bowman offered four Sabres for Coffey. But Sather held his ground. His steadfastness is now paying off.

With Gretzky leading the charge, the Oilers easily have the highest-scoring team in the league. In a sport in which scoring 40 goals is like hitting 25 home runs, the Edmonton lineup is Murderers' Row. Gretzky and Messier, who already has 36 goals, are the heaviest hitters, and Anderson (27), Coffey (26), Kurri (23) and Dave Lumley (23) also are on pace for 30 goals or more. Looking at it another way, Detroit's leading scorer, Mark Osborne, has 16 goals and 34 assists for 50 points; were he at Edmonton, he would be the *number 7* scorer.

The Oilers pretty much have all the parts. The prolific offense is balanced by such veteran defensemen as Doug Hicks, Lee Fogolin and Garry Lariviere, who stay at home, and by rugged forwards Pat Hughes and Dave Hunter, who held Montreal's famed Guy Lafleur to no goals in last year's playoffs. And though Gretzky and the other scorers might seem like inviting targets, they rarely are hit. Pesky and elusive, Gretzky says only twice in his life has he been banged hard enough to see stars. "Hit him?" says Nanne. "You can't hit Gretzky with a handful of confetti."

Besides, Curt Brackenbury, a human pinball on ice, and, especially, Dave Semenko stand ever ready to protect him. At 6'3", 215 pounds, Semenko, 24, was once the undefeated heavyweight champ of the WHA. He's disliked by rival teams, who mockingly call him "cement head," and not even all that much admired by Oiler owner Peter Pocklington, who once said Semenko skates "like a Zamboni." But Semenko knows his role as one of the league's most unsavory players. He once smashed the face of Islander Goalie Billy Smith so hard that Smith's mask flew over the glass into the stands. "I've seen it a couple of times with us," says Vancouver Coach Harry Neale. "Gretzky just kind of rolls his head in the direction of a guy who just hit him, and Semenko moves in."

While the Oilers' blue-line corps is sound, the heart of any defense is in the nets, and Edmonton's goaltending is superior. That's because at last June's draft Sather broke NHL tradition by selecting a goalie, Grant Fuhr, in the first round. Fuhr stepped right in as the No. 1 goalkeeper. He has lost only three of 33 decisions, and from Oct. 14 until Jan. 16 he went 24 games without a defeat. Fuhr is a standup shot-blocker with keen reflexes and an uncommon knack for steering deflections toward his teammates. His play has been good enough to make him – along with Messier,

Coffey and Gretzky – an All-Star. To top that all off, Fuhr is only 19 – and he's black.

Adopted by a white couple as an infant, Fuhr grew up outside of Edmonton in Spruce Grove, Alberta. Though he's only the seventh black player in NHL history – and the first to tend goal – Fuhr isn't on any kind of racial crusade. He'd much rather be compared with Ken Dryden than with Jackie Robinson. "It's more interesting," he says. Still, one day might he not enjoy his historic significance? "Not really."

"Grant, do you get excited about anything?"

"Not really."

"Why not?"

"There's not a whole lot to get excited about."

Fortunately for the Oilers, if not for newsmen, Fuhr is as impenetrable in goal as he is in the interview room. "I've never seen anyone like him," Sather says. "He never gets rattled or shakes his head or panics." Adds Lumley, "A puck may have just whizzed by his head, and all Grant will say is, 'Hmm, that was an interesting shot.'"

Last season, while playing junior hockey for Victoria, British Columbia, Fuhr gave up 2.78 goals a game, the least in the Western Hockey League. Normally, junior teams alternate two or more goalies. Thus, draft-age netminders tend to be woefully inexperienced. Not Fuhr. He was so exceptional that Victoria Coach Jack Shupe started him in 59 of 72 games. In his sales pitch to Sather, Barry Fraser, the Oilers' chief scout, called Fuhr the most promising junior goaltender since Bernie Parent. At the moment, he's the leading candidate for Rookie of the Year.

Teammates may tease Fuhr about his lack of loquaciousness, but that's nothing compared with the treatment they give Gretzky, whom they constantly needle, particularly about the size of his nose. He may be The Great One or Mr. Waynederful elsewhere and to others, yet in the Edmonton locker room he's Wheeze – short for Weasel. But while the Oilers razz him and say he's merely their equal, they are all in awe of his talent. "What amazes me most is that he never stops amazing me," says Messier. "He'll do some totally incredible thing and you think, 'O.K., that's it; I'll never see the likes of that again.' Then, damn, he does something even more incredible."

To illustrate, Messier points to a five-game stretch last December. In the first four games, Gretzky sort of hit for the cycle – only in goals – scoring three, two, one and then four. Messier thought, "What can he possibly do for an encore?" Gretzky showed him in the very next game, against defensively strong Philadelphia. Gretzky got *five* goals. Most astonishingly, the five-goal spree raised his season total to 50. Only two other players in NHL history, Maurice Richard in 1944–45 and Mike Bossy last year, have scored 50 goals in 50 games, and both needed all 50 games. For Gretzky, goal number 50 came in Game 39.

Afterward, the Flyers' Bobby Clarke and Paul Holmgren violated an NHL taboo by visiting an opponent's locker room. "I know everything's been written about you," Clarke told Gretzky. "I think none of it is adequate." Two weeks ago, another familiar face popped into the Oiler locker room and asked Gretzky if he could please have an autographed hockey stick. It was Orr.

Much has been said about Gretzky's early on-ice training, about his dad, Walter, sailing pucks around a flooded backyard rink for little Wayne to chase. But the fact remains, most NHL players practiced hard as kids, and none of them is as good as Gretzky. "The idea that Wayne is the player he is because of how hard he worked is garbage," says Sather. "What he does on the ice isn't taught; it comes down straight from the Lord."

Sather's chief concern, naturally, is keeping Gretzky's skates on the ice. "His presence alone psychs out our opponents," says Sather. "My job is to manipulate Wayne so that he upsets them as much as possible, without wearing him down." Still, Sather regularly calls upon Gretzky to take abnormally long, 1½-to-two-minute shifts, which means he plays 32 to 38 minutes a game. Most first-line centers are on the ice about 22 minutes. Sather also "floats" Gretzky at center with all four sets of wings almost every game. At times Sather has even played Gretzky at wing and once used him as a defenseman. Last week, in a 6–3 loss to Montreal, Canadien Center Doug Risebrough was assigned to cover Gretzky, but Wayne's manipulations nearly drove Risebrough batty. At one point Risebrough went off the ice, on again, off, and on again – all in about 10 seconds. He was leaping over the boards like a man jumping rope, until Referee Andy Van Hellemondfinally resolved his dilemma by whistling him to the bench.

Sather has no problem assigning linemates to Gretzky. All the Oilers practically beg for ice time with him. "Playing with Wayne's a career break," says Kurri. "With him, you know your plus-minus, goals and assists will go up." Adds Anderson, "He opens up the game, lifts the action to a higher level. He makes hockey more fun." In all, Gretzky has set up 14 different teammates for goals this season. Of the Oilers' 313 goals, he has scored or assisted on 152. He has gotten points in 52 games. In the six he hasn't, Edmonton's record is 1–4–1.

"Wayne's like having your own Fantasy Island," says Lumley, who should know. In November, Sather put Lumley on a line with Gretzky, and Lumley immediately went on a 12-game goal-scoring streak, one short of the modern record set by the Kings' Charlie Simmer in 1980–81. Right before the streak, Lumley had spent 13 games in the stands.

When Gretzky assumes control of the puck, Edmonton's Northlands Coliseum – or any other NHL arena, for that matter – crackles with electricity. He likes to set up in the 10-foot area behind the enemy goal line and quarterback the offense from there. Bowman says that from behind the goal Gretzky has such complete vision his passing becomes uncanny. "He's the only player I've ever seen who can consistently center the puck from there through three sets of skates – and softly," says Bowman.

According to Edmonton's backup goalie, Ron Low, Gretzky invented a behind-the-net shot whereby he blasts the puck off the heel of the goalie's stick so that it caroms into the net. He actually practices this play and has scored off it several times in games. Against Hartford last year, Gretzky was trapped behind the net, defensemen barreling toward him from both sides. Kurri was open in the slot. Gretzky flipped the puck onto the blade of his stick and flicked it over the goal – a perfect pass – and Kurri tapped it home. "I never saw *that* before," says Low. "Not even in practice."

Talent, leadership, savvy – all of these qualities combine in Gretzky with a deep, smoldering drive never to be beaten. "Wayne has simply got to be first," says Fogolin. "With him there's no other way. If someone takes the puck from him, he starts to get red spots on his face, and he becomes very intent. You know next time out he'll go like the wind, lift the tempo a notch. And if everybody keeps up with him, he'll lift it more, and more...until he feels he's gotten even." Gretzky doesn't deny this. "Hockey is supposed to be fun," he says, "but it's fun only when you're winning."

Being the best has made Gretzky rich, even though in his first two NHL seasons he didn't get all the money he might have. He was content with a salary of about $150,000 a year, despite reports that other NHL stars, notably Los Angeles' Marcel Dionne, were making close to $600,000. But before this season began he had a long talk with Pocklington, and two weeks ago Gretzky emerged with a 21-year deal. The first 15 years could be worth $20 million.

Interestingly, Gretzky shied away from any of the incentive clauses such contracts normally contain. "I believe that I sign a contract to do my best," he says. "I should be paid for that, not for scoring 20 goals or 90 goals." In place of such sweeteners, however, Gretzky's contract calls for extra money if the team does well, with increments for making the playoffs and then for each round it wins in them. Gretzky loves the arrangement. "I'm not *the* Edmonton Oilers," he says. "I'm part of the team." News of the contract also has enhanced Gretzky's image as a rising media star, replete with a fast-growing following of ogling fans and an ever-increasing entourage of newspeople from Canada and the U.S.

This is beginning to cause some strain. Despite his unflagging politeness, last week Gretzky began dodging interview requests for the first time. The day before the Montreal game, he snapped at Oiler publicity man Bill Tuele, "What else can they possibly ask me? I've told them everything I know." But calls keep coming, as many as 100 a day, including one last week from a woman in Los Angeles. "Where's that Wayne?" she asked Tuele. "He's such a cutie. I just want to rape him." The next day, the Oilers announced that all Gretzky interviews must be done in the locker room.

In part, the arrangement is designed to help avoid a repeat of a five-game winless streak Edmonton went through on a road trip in mid-January. All told, 132 reporters requested interviews with Gretzky during that Eastern swing. Between the media crush and playing five games in five different cities in seven nights, Gretzky was pale and tired. At one point he told Allen Abel of the Toronto *Globe and Mail*, "I bleed, too. People think my day lasts 30 hours. Years ago, my father used to tell me, 'Either go out and practice now or you'll be getting up at six in the morning the rest of your life to go to work.' Now I'm getting up at 5:30 to catch airplanes. We laugh about that a lot."

Last week Gretzky was still laughing. So were the Oilers.

Gretzky ended the 1981–82 season with 92 goals – a record that remains untouched to this day – and became the first player to score over 200 points, having ended the season with 212.

GREATNESS CONFIRMED

BY E.M. SWIFT | DECEMBER 27, 1982

*Four of the best players in NHL history – Ken Dryden,
Phil Esposito, Bobby Orr and Gordie Howe – assessed the
supremacy of Wayne Gretzky*

(Photograph by Brian Lanker)

HE MAY BE THE MOST PRECOCIOUS ATHLETE OF OUR TIME.
At six Wayne Gretzky was competing against 10-year-olds; at 16 he was dominating 20-year-olds; at 17 he was the youngest athlete playing a major league sport in North America; and at 20 he broke the NHL single-season scoring record. "I've always done everything early," says Gretzky.

As youngsters, most athletes who become superstars are blessed not only with extraordinary coordination but also with other physical advantages, such as exceptional size, strength and speed. All they lack are experience and the insight that derives from it. Gretzky, on the other hand, has been, as Longfellow wrote of Hiawatha, "learned in all the lore of old men" since his early teens. His speed was average, his size and strength below average, but his coordination and aptitude for his sport were so advanced that by the time he was 19 he had proved himself to be the best hockey player in the world. Still, as he matured physically, there was more to come.

Last season, at 21, Gretzky put together a year that no one in hockey had thought possible: 92 goals and 120 assists for 212 points in 80 games. These totals are so far beyond the previous records that they're difficult to put in perspective. It's as if some kid suddenly hit 78 home runs, passing 60 by mid-August. Our sense of history was offended. The NHL's second-leading scorer last season, Mike Bossy, had the fourth-highest point total (147) in league history, but he trailed Gretzky by 65 points. That's half a season's work for most big scorers.

The last time anyone wreaked so much havoc on his sport's record book was in 1961–62, when Wilt Chamberlain led the NBA in scoring with a 50.4 average, 12 points higher than the previous mark. Walt Bellamy, the league's No. 2 scorer in 1961–62, had a 31.6 average. But Chamberlain's feat was understandable. He was a phenomenal physical specimen, 7 feet tall, enormously strong, marvelously coordinated. Furthermore, he had a coach who told Wilt's Philadelphia Warrior teammates to feed, feed, feed him the ball. Gretzky is as normally proportioned as the newspaperboy. He's a shade under 6 feet tall and weighs 172 pounds – and not a particularly muscular 172 pounds, either. Gretzky registered last in strength evaluations conducted by his team, the Edmonton Oilers, in 1981. "He tests very normally in other areas, too," says Glen Sather, the Oilers' coach and general manager. "I think he runs totally on adrenaline."

Gretzky certainly doesn't run on iron. When his blood was tested near the end of last season, he was found to be close to anemia. Yet there he was playing with a bunch of guys like Lumley and Kurri and Callighen – talented players but hardly stars – and taking us to scoring heights never imagined. Along the way this nearly anemic wunderkind-next-door shattered Rocket Richard's mark of 50 goals in 50 games, probably the most hallowed record in hockey. It had stood since 1945 and had been equaled only once, by Bossy in 1980–81. Gretzky, who sets up many more goals than he scores, many more than Richard or Bossy ever set up, got his 50th goal last season in his 39th game. Afterward, Richard, who seldom praises modern players, said, "I have now seen Gretzky enough to say that in whatever decade he played, he would've been the scoring champion."

Gretzky now holds 27 individual NHL records. Gordie Howe is next with 14. Gretzky has been in the league three years, and three times he has been its Most Valuable Player. (He played one season, 1978–79, in the WHA and was its Rookie of the Year.) Yet he has remained unchanged and respectful through it all, almost awed by those players whose achievements he has been surpassing. He's the young champion hockey so badly needs.

BOBBY ORR SITS IN THE UPSTAIRS STUDY OF HIS HOME IN Weston, Mass. Ten years ago he was hockey's champion, its wunderkind, although he didn't relish the limelight as Gretzky does. No one has ever controlled the flow of the game as did Orr, who's the only player other than Gretzky to have had more than 100 assists in a season. Now 34, Orr has been retired for four years, his astounding career cut short by a series of knee injuries. He represents Nabisco Brands, traveling around the country to make personal appearances and give youth hockey clinics. With that curious loyalty that former hockey stars feel toward their sport – even if the sport has hurt them – Orr cares deeply about the future of the game, the kids. "How do you look after a house?" he asks. "The foundation. We're not looking after our foundation."

It has been suggested that Gretzky, like Orr, like many of the great ones, must see the game at a slower speed than the rest of us. You hear of batters who can see the stitches on a ball before they hit it. Orr, asked about this, smiles. "That's too deep for me," he says. "I'm sure Wayne does things there's no darn way he can explain. I know I did. I remember one game I played against Montreal when the puck bounced into the air near the boards. I just swung at it. I didn't know what else to do. The puck went right into the corner of the net. You think I planned that?" He laughs. "You don't explain things like that.

"To me what makes Wayne different is the little things. Not big technical things. His strengths are fundamental. He's not real fast, but he's faster than you think. He doesn't have Bobby Hull's shot, but he shoots better than you think. He passes better than anybody I've ever seen. And he thinks so far ahead. There was one game last January, against St. Louis, when Gretzky was coming down on the left wing. The right wing had the puck." Orr pauses here, smiling at the difficulty of describing the play. He stands up and walks across the study to grab a hockey stick leaning against the wall. "The right wing passes Gretzky the puck, only it's behind Wayne," says Orr. "The defenseman in front of Gretzky straightens up. Only instead of reaching back for the pass the way the rest of us would have done [Orr now reaches awkwardly behind him with his stick, making himself easy prey for the imaginary defenseman], Gretzky keeps skating. The puck skitters off the boards and past the defenseman, and Wayne's looking back for it now. He picks it up and is on his way. I'm sitting there saying, 'That's what makes him different.' He keeps things simple. That to me was the highlight of the game.

"People keep waiting for him to fall on his face, but as long as he doesn't tire mentally, he'll play the game. That's my only fear, that he'll get mentally worn out. Wayne does many, many more things off the ice – appearances, endorsements – than I ever did. I did what I thought was my fair share, but it wasn't my thing. I just hope he has good people around him who are watching him. He's young and full of energy, and when you have that, you feel you can do it all forever. But hockey can't afford to lose its Gretzkys." Orr says this without a trace of bitterness. "Hockey would have survived the last three years without him; hockey will always *survive*. But if Wayne is influencing the hundreds of thousands, the millions of kids that I think he is – well, put it this way: Thank God he's around."

The NHL has always subscribed to the theory that violence sells. Indeed, it *has* sold. Philadelphia, the most penalized team in the league each of the past 11 seasons, also has been the league's top drawing card on the road since 1976–77. Inevitably, the Flyers' popularity has affected youngsters who play the game. Monkey see, monkey do. The results can be seen at any youth or high school hockey game. Kids, protected by mandatory face masks, skate around like little *kamikaze* pilots, sticks held at head level, elbows flying, the natural grace of the sport lost in the near-mayhem.

Enter Gretzky, who has averaged just 24 minutes of penalties a season in his pro career and who uses his stick solely to manipulate the puck, as was originally intended. Does that sell? In 1979–80, Edmonton's first year in the NHL, the Oilers were the worst road draw in the league, playing before 71.3% of capacity. Last season, however, the Gretzky magic took hold. Edmonton was third in road attendance, drawing 88.7% of capacity. The Oilers' last 17 away games were sellouts. In two appearances in Detroit, home of the hapless Red Wings, Gretzky's Oilers attracted the largest (20,628) and third-largest regular-season crowds in NHL history. And Edmonton led the league in road attendance through the first quarter of the 1982–83 season despite a middling 9–7–4 record. The fans are coming to see Gretzky. Artistry sells.

Says Orr, "It takes some time before the professional influence filters down to the kids, but it does filter down."

To the foundation.

IT'S THE NIGHT OF NOV. 14, AND PHIL ESPOSITO IS IN THE television broadcast booth high above the ice in Madison Square Garden. Esposito now does color commentary for New York Ranger games, and tonight the Rangers are hosting the Oilers. Like Gretzky, Esposito, 40, was a center, and during his 18-year career he had 717 goals and 873 assists while playing for Chicago, Boston and the Rangers. Only Howe got more career goals and points. Espo's best years were with the Bruins, for whom he had 76 goals and 76 assists in 1970–71. Those 76 goals and 152 points were NHL single-season records until Gretzky came along. In a funny way, Esposito had been expecting him.

"When Wayne Gretzky was 16, he played for the junior Greyhounds in the Soo," says Esposito, referring to his hometown of Sault Ste. Marie, Ont. "My dad owned a piece of the team, and he called me one day on the phone. 'Phil,' he said, 'I saw a kid who's going to break all your records.' 'Oh yeah?' I said. 'Who is this kid?' 'Wayne Gretzky. Believe me, he's as good as Orr was.' Well, I'd heard of him, but for crying out loud he was 16 years old. But my father's always been right when it comes to judging talent, so I started following Wayne. I never had the God-given talent of Wayne Gretzky. The only guy who had that was Bobby Orr. They're in a class by themselves, but it takes guts to recognize that you have that talent and dedicate yourself to it."

For the Ranger game Gretzky is playing on a line with Jari Kurri and Jaroslav Pouzar. Sather uses Gretzky with many different sets of wings, and it's a measure of Gretzky's remarkable skills that he can adapt to whoever is out there with him. When Esposito set his records in 1970–71, three other Bruins rounded out the league's top four in scoring – Johnny Bucyk, Ken Hodge and Orr. Gretzky had no such supporting cast last season. No other Oilers were among the top 10 scorers, yet as a team Edmonton set a record for most goals in a season (417). Gretzky either scored or assisted on better than half of them.

In the first period against the Rangers Gretzky breaks in on goal, two-on-one, and threads a pass to Pouzar through a defenseman's legs. Pouzar, shooting on an open net, hits the post. "Did you see how soft Gretzky put that pass on his stick?" Esposito asks the TV audience. Later, when Kurri takes a shot from the right wing, Gretzky breaks immediately to the left boards. The shot misses the net, and the puck caroms directly onto Gretzky's stick. "Did you see what he did then?" Esposito says. "Most players would have gone straight to the net, but Gretzky knew that nine times out of 10 either that shot was going to miss the net or the goalie would kick the rebound to the left side. That's why he's as great as he is. He's so smart."

Halfway through the second period, Gretzky has two goals and an assist. Esposito sounds like a Gretzky cheerleader, and he doesn't have to work to summon his enthusiasm. He turns to Jim Gordon, the Rangers' play-by-play man, and asks rhetorically, "O.K., it's 4–2 Oilers, and Gretzky has three points. Do you say the heck with the fans and follow him around now?"

In other words, should the Rangers shadow Gretzky, a ploy that's often effective but is unpopular with many hockey fans who resent seeing Gretzky or any star stifled by a defensive specialist. The only team to have shadowed Gretzky successfully so far is Boston, which uses a young center named Steve Kasper for the job. Kasper was voted the best defensive forward in the NHL last season largely because he held Gretzky to a total of one goal and four assists in three games. In the two games the Bruins and the Oilers have played against each other so far this year, Gretzky has gotten only three assists. Shadowing is a trend to which Gretzky will soon grow accustomed.

"He doesn't try to be a one-man show," says Kasper, "and he doesn't have to carry the puck to be effective. It only takes him an instant to do what he wants with it. The main thing I try to do is keep him on the outside of the ice and nudge him early to get him off his stride, like a bump and run in football. It's no good trying to line him up for a hard check; he's too mobile. If you start lunging at him, he'll make you look ridiculous. One thing I'll never call him is a floater. He wants the puck and he'll check to get it. Gretzky's a complete player."

"Gretzky's very underrated defensively," says Esposito during a break. "These people who say he can't play defense don't know what they're talking about. He knows when he has to be back deep in his zone and when he doesn't. He knows when his defenseman's going to be beat before his defenseman knows it."

Late in the third period Edmonton leads the Rangers 6–2. The New York fans, as coarse a lot as has ever graced an arena, are bored with booing their team and have begun to cheer Gretzky, who, shadowless, has been putting on a dazzling show. Suddenly he and Pouzar break down the ice two-on-two, Gretzky carrying the puck. He cuts to his left, in front of Pouzar and tantalizingly close to the Ranger defensemen, who both pick him up. Gretzky then flips the puck back to Pouzar, who has darted into the hole vacated by Gretzky's defender. "Look at him," says Esposito. "Oh my." Pouzar skates in alone and scores the game's final goal. The Ranger fans cheer.

Artistry sells. Even on Broadway.

WITHOUT MUCH DOUBT, GRETZKY'S MOST SHOCKING FEAT last season was his 92 goals. Even though he had scored 51 and 55 goals, respectively, in his first two years in the NHL, Gretzky was known primarily as a playmaker. He liked to set up behind the net and pass to teammates as they broke toward the goal, a tactic that opposing teams began to go to great lengths to prevent. "It got to the point where defensemen would go behind the net and wait for me," says

Gretzky. "So last season I started moving out to the slot more, and in the first 20 games I started shooting all the time."

And with uncanny accuracy. While Esposito needed 550 shots to score 76 goals, Gretzky got his 76th on his 287th shot. He scored his 92 goals on just 369 shots for an accuracy percentage of 24.9%. Broken down, 22 of Gretzky's goals were scored in the first period, 30 in the second and 40 in the third – a testament to his remarkable stamina. In the playoffs the Oilers, who had finished second in the overall standings (48–17–15), were upset by the 17th-place Los Angeles Kings (24–41–15) in five games. Edmonton lost one game 10–8 and another 6–5 after leading 5–0. The defense caved in. Gretzky had five goals and seven assists in the series, or 2.4 points per game, only slightly below his regular-season average of 2.65. The next morning he flew to the World Championships in Helsinki, where he was the leading scorer with 14 points in 10 games.

"People said I was tired at the end of the year, and they thought that was one reason we lost to the Kings," says Gretzky, who last season averaged a whopping 38 minutes of ice time a game, killing penalties and working the power play in addition to his regular shifts, which frequently run three minutes apiece, compared with perhaps a minute for mere mortals. "But in that last game of the year, maybe the 100th I'd played that season, I had three goals and two assists against Sweden. How could I have been tired?"

TWO NIGHTS AFTER THE RANGER GAME, ON NOV. 16, KEN Dryden is in the stands at the Nassau Coliseum to see the Oilers play the New York Islanders. Dryden was the premier goaltender of the 1970s. During his eight seasons with Montreal, the Canadiens won the Stanley Cup six times. His 2.24 career goals-against average is the lowest in the league since 1941. He retired in 1979, four months before Gretzky broke into the NHL. Dryden, 35, a non-practicing lawyer, now lives in Toronto and is completing a book on hockey. This will be the third time he has watched Gretzky play in person.

"The thing about Gretzky," says Dryden, "is that unlike most other great goal scorers, he's a real sniper – Bossy's another one – much like the Europeans. He doesn't miss much. The other great ones – Hull, Esposito, Richard, Howe – were volume shooters. They were quite stoppable, but they created so many scoring chances that they ended up with a lot of goals.

"The other thing I've noticed is that Gretzky has discovered the top of the net. An awful lot of his goals are top corner goals. Traditionally players were told to shoot low because of rebounds and because hands move better than feet. That's true, except hands have farther to move. When I played I was operating on a 3-foot-high net."

The goal cage, then as now, is 4 feet high. If Dryden played a 3-foot-high net, he essentially conceded the top corners – because few shooters ever aimed there. He believes the predilection for the low shot may well have stemmed from the mid-1960s, when Stan Mikita and Hull were pioneering the curved stick and 100-mph slap shot. "A lot of goalies then didn't wear masks, or the masks were very primitive," says Dryden. "So day after day in practice there were tantrums and things like that by goalies if someone shot high. Their outrage was quite legitimate. Injuries from high shots back then would have been very, very serious. So with their coaches and goalies all yelling at them, players didn't practice shooting high. Slowly goalies' crouches got lower and lower as they tried to cover the bottom corners. That left the top corners more and more exposed." Which Gretzky has exploited.

The game begins, and seven minutes into the first period Gretzky sets up Kurri for a power-play goal that ties the score 1–1. "Everything developed so quickly," says Dryden, impressed with Gretzky's pass. "The puck didn't stay on his stick. Once you beat someone, if you move the puck quickly you don't allow him back in the play. He stays beaten."

Later, Gretzky tries the opposite tactic, skating down the wing and waiting, waiting, waiting for someone to break free. "He has an enormous sense of patience," says Dryden. "Everybody has a moment of panic, but Gretzky's comes so much later than other players'. When he comes down the ice, there's a point when the defenseman thinks: He's going to commit himself one way or the other now. When that moment passes and Gretzky still hasn't committed, the whole rhythm of the game is upset. The defenseman is unprepared for what might come next. It's not an anticlimax. It's *beyond* the climax. And suddenly a player becomes open who wasn't open a moment before."

Dryden is enjoying the game. It's fast and crisp, with good action at both ends. "I remember when I played against Esposito and the puck went out of the corner, I always assumed it was going onto Espo's stick, and that it would then be coming my way," he says. "With Gretzky, a goalie just has to assume that when Wayne passes the puck out from behind the net, it's going onto a stick and there will then be a shot. You can't commit yourself to Gretzky the way you could to other great goal scorers because when you can move the puck as well as he can, well, there's no reason to shoot very often. Which, of course, works to his advantage."

By the third period the Islanders lead 4–2. Butch Goring, who has been covering Gretzky, has done a good job. By bumping Gretzky off stride, tugging at his arm discreetly, Goring has thrown him off his game. Several times Islander checkers have sent Gretzky sprawling. "I don't think he's going to get hurt often," says Dryden. "He's never really committed to any one direction, which makes him a hard person to injure. His body is always moving in a number of ways. In Orr, you sensed more power, more commitment. Gretzky will just sort of collapse in the direction you hit him."

There's a faint smile on Dryden's face. "He's a much better skater than I thought he was," he says. "He's just not a pretty skater. I never realized he was so quick." Gretzky is chasing one of the Islander defenders, who's trying to move the puck. "He's always pressing, but when you think of someone who's relentless, there's usually something very heavy-handed about it. Gretzky's almost spritelike." The puck is now along the boards, and Gretzky is circling in center ice, away from the play. "There's almost a will-of-the-wisp quality to the way he skates. He's very light. There's such a sense of freedom about him. There don't seem to be any constraints."

A LIGHT SNOW IS FALLING IN EDMONTON ON THE NIGHT OF Dec. 1. Gretzky has had one or more goals or assists every game this season, and tonight his two assists will pull him within one game of the consecutive-game scoring record of 28 held by Montreal's Guy Lafleur. Four nights later he will break Lafleur's mark. The streak will finally end at 30 against Los Angeles on Dec. 9.

Gretzky has picked up this season where he left off in 1981–82: He's running away with the league scoring championship. As of Dec. 18, he was averaging 2.51 points a game and was tied for second in the NHL in goals with 26. He had more goals (34) at the same point last year but fewer assists (48 to 57). Gretzky says teams have taken the front of the net away from him again, so he has moved back behind it, from where he's content to pass to teammates. "A lot of my game depends on how the other team is playing me," he says.

Tonight the Oilers' opponents are the Flyers, who this season have changed their style from a bullying team to a skating one. The game will start at 7:35, and three minutes before it begins, as one of the national anthems is being sung, Bobby Hull arrives. He's out of breath from climbing the arena stairs, but he's grinning, his broad, scarred face bursting with energy. He's also sweating. "I thought we were going to be a minute late, and Wayne would have a couple of goals already," he says, beaming. A friend, Bill Urzada, has met Hull, who lives in Demorestville, Ont., at the Edmonton airport and driven him to the Coliseum. Both raise registered polled Herefords.

Hull, the first man to score more than 50 goals in a season, may be the player most responsible for hockey as we know it today. As great as Howe was, as great as Orr, Esposito and Beliveau were, they didn't have Hull's charisma. His style of play exactly matched his personality – open, dramatic, uncompromising and utterly joyful. People paid to see him play, and they departed feeling they had shared something pretty good. "A lot of times those Chicago fans left the rink as tired as we were," recalls Hull. "When it's a great game, you can't believe it when it's over, and you can't wait for the next game to start.

"I liked to entertain. I loved playing the way I thought the game should be played. I knew people wanted to see me take that biscuit and go with it." Hull is grinning as he says this, eyes glinting. His voice is raspy and full of laughter. "Wayne's got that same attitude. He thinks of himself as an entertainer, and the more he entertains, the more packed houses he'll draw, the more franchises will be kept alive, the more players will have work, and the more money everyone will make. It's no strain on him to give as much as he does to the game, off the ice and on. Any strain is overcome by the joy of doing well. Look at him. He doesn't want to come off the ice. That's another thing that sets him apart. He comes to play every game. He *likes* to perform."

Gretzky is killing a penalty early in the game and steals the puck from the Flyers' captain, Bill Barber. Gretzky skates in by himself on a breakaway and takes his stick back, pausing at the top of his swing, upsetting the natural rhythm of the play. When he finally slaps the shot, it ricochets off the post and wide of the net. Hull winces. "I never liked to go in alone," he says. "Too much time to think about it." Then he turns, surprised. "You find yourself pulling for him, don't you?"

Gretzky is behind the net on an Edmonton power play as two players scrap for the puck along the boards. "He's not chasing the puck, not out in traffic where a guy can hit him," says Hull. "His linemates know where he is, and they can just blindly throw the puck behind the net. When the puck hits his stick it stays there. A lot of these guys have skinny little blades that the puck is always bouncing over, but Gretzky's got a big stick and a big blade, too."

Gretzky, as Hull did, tapes his blade all the way from toe to heel and then rubs baby powder into the tape to reduce its tackiness. Without the powder the puck feels sluggish on the stick. "I've noticed that when the puck comes off the boards, it's usually spinning very quickly," says Gretzky. "My first year in the league I didn't use any tape, and the puck kept sliding off the end of my stick. The cushion the tape provides helps stop the spin."

In the second period, Gretzky sets up Kurri for a short-handed goal, and later he assists Pat Hughes on a power-play goal. Hull is laughing. "See what he did?" he says. "He gave it to Hughes before he ever saw Hughes. He knows where everyone is at all times. I could *kick* in 25 goals a year if I played with Gretzky.

"Hockey needed a shot in the arm when he came along. It needed a champion. People are again relating to hockey as a game of skill, because that's the way Wayne plays. We were getting away from that. Scouts had been forgetting about the goals-assists-points column and, because of the success of the Flyers, going right to the columns that told about total penalty minutes and size. 'Ah-ha! This guy's an intimidator.' So he's drafted. But now they're looking for goals and assists again."

Gretzky is knocked down for the umpteenth time but gets to his feet and, relentlessly, begins chasing the puck carrier again, trying to score the tying goal. Hull, still brawny and powerful at 43, is shaking his head, not quite able to accept this flaw in Gretzky's style, this penchant for getting knocked on his can. "I just never wanted to fall," says Hull. "I thought it was a sin to get knocked down."

Suddenly Gretzky slaps the puck out of the air and is stickhandling along the boards, looking for an opening. Edmonton, behind 3–2 in the final minute, has pulled its goalie for a sixth attacker. Gretzky is trying to make a play that will never unfold. "Just look at him," Hull says, grinning in admiration. "The puck is *glued* to him. On the two teams, taking nothing away from the rest of the guys, who in the hell else out there do you want to look at but Gretzky?"

No one else. He's sharing something with us that's pretty good.

The 1982–83 season proved to be a step back for Gretzky over the previous year; he ended it with only 196 points. The "slump" was short lived; he scored over 200 points in each of the next three seasons.

MAN WITH A STREAK OF SHEER GENIUS

BY JACK FALLA | JANUARY 23, 1984

*Wayne Gretzky scored at least one point in the first
46 games of the 1983–84 season, breaking his old record and
leaving the hockey world wondering how long it would last*
(Photograph by Manny Millan)

HUMOR HIM, I SAID TO MYSELF ON THAT FEBRUARY morning in 1974 when my father phoned from Quebec City, where he was coaching the Boston Junior Braves in the annual International Pee Wee Hockey Tournament. Let his enthusiasm spend itself unopposed by my common sense.

"Do you know any college coaches who'd like to win about four NCAA championships?" my father had asked.

I said that he must have been out looking at the 16- to 19-year-olds in the Canadian junior leagues.

"No. This one's a Pee Wee," he said. "He just turned 13. His father says he might go to college if he doesn't turn pro. The boy could be the best thing since Orr." That sounded compelling, until my father explained that, no, the kid wasn't that strong or fast or possessed of a particularly hard shot.

"What can he do?" I asked.

"He's a genius at scoring goals."

I asked who he was.

"Wayne Gretzky," my father said. "Remember his name."

"Say 'hi' to Mom," I said, instantly forgetting the name but remembering what I thought was my father's curious use of the word genius.

It is now nine years and 11 months since I first heard the name Gretzky and looked at the snapshots my parents had taken in Quebec, pictures that show a thin boy with a fragile angularity of face. The only thing about him that bespoke athleticism was his seemingly too-large team jacket.

I recently recalled all this while riding an elevator up 17 floors to Gretzky's six-room duplex penthouse in Edmonton.

Gretzky, framed by his doorway, is a portrait in black and white – soft black leather shoes, white socks, black leather pants, black shirt and blond hair cut shorter than he wore it last year. He has a pasty complexion and a wide, even smile accented by a rather pointy nose. Out of his Edmonton Oilers number 99 uniform, Gretzky looks more like an actor or a rock singer than what he has become – the greatest offensive force in the history of hockey and one of the greatest athletes in all sport. He is, truly, a goal-scoring genius. Not quite 23 (his birthday is Jan. 26) and now in his sixth year of professional hockey (fifth in the NHL), Gretzky already ranks 27th among the NHL's alltime scorers. If he gets 207 points this season – by Sunday he was ahead of that pace with 136 points on 53 goals, 83 assists with 34 regular-season games left – he will move past Bobby Orr, who is currently in 22nd place on the alltime list. And at his career scoring rate of 2.315 points per game, Gretzky would pass Gordie Howe to become hockey's alltime leading scorer sometime in the 1988–89 season, accomplishing in ten seasons what took Howe 26.

Gretzky holds or shares 34 NHL records and is a virtual lock to win his fourth consecutive NHL scoring title. His statistics this season make him a dot on the horizon to even his nearest pursuer, his linemate Jari Kurri, who leads the Mere Mortals Division with 39 goals and 46 assists. Many of Kurri's points have come because he plays on Gretzky's right wing.

But none of Gretzky's other stats have the astonishing immediacy of The Streak. After Sunday's 5–4 Edmonton win over the Devils in New Jersey, Gretzky had scored at least one point in all 46 games this season. To put that in perspective, the previous record was 30 consecutive games, set by Gretzky last season after he broke Guy Lafleur's record of 28.

"It's so hard to compare that with anything in hockey," says Michael Barnett, president of CorpSport International, the marketing company which handles Gretzky's product endorsements and other business affairs, "that what we're starting to see is people, especially in the States, comparing it with Joe DiMaggio's 56-game hitting streak in 1941."

Gretzky thinks that is like comparing apples to oranges (or pucks to baseballs). "DiMaggio got up to bat only four or five times per game, and he could have been walked," he says. "His fate wasn't completely in his hands. I know I'll get five or six shifts per period. I get more chances."

"But nobody guarantees him a shot on goal," says Glen Sather, the Oiler's coach and general manager, who feels the streaks are "very comparable from the historical point of their being so much more than what anyone else in either sport ever did."

Then there are those who think Gretzky's streak may be an even greater accomplishment than DiMaggio's. Indeed, a hit doesn't always result in a run, but a goal or an assist always puts a point on the board.

Gretzky won't admit it, but Barnett and others close to the player say he harbors a secret goal of getting at least one point in all 80 games, an achievement that might not be comparable to anything in major professional sports.

"I'm just having fun with it," says Gretzky. "I felt a little pressure to break 30, but after that I just said, 'Hey, this is fun. I wonder how long it can last?'"

After a tour of his bright, airy penthouse, Gretzky walks into a hall where there are two large framed prints of Andy Warhol paintings, one of Marilyn Monroe, the other a self-portrait. Gretzky met Warhol in New York last summer and posed for photographs, one of which Warhol used as the basis for six paintings. One of the paintings will go to Gretzky – "I'm putting it over the grand piano" – while the other five will be sold, probably for $30,000 each.

As unlikely as it seems, Gretzky and Warhol have become friends. "I think it's great when a sports star can look like a movie star," says Warhol in reference to the fact that Gretzky spent part of last summer in Hollywood taping guest appearances on several television shows. That's the superficial Gretzky. Warhol focuses in on the essential Gretzky when he says, "As an artist, what I see in Wayne is great joy and energy."

Indeed, Gretzky plays not with the driving power of Orr or the Gallic passion of Lafleur but with a shorebird's sprightliness, flitting in lines and arcs that often seem unrelated to the flow of play until, suddenly, he and the puck are at the same place at the same time.

That joyful coming together was conspicuous on the night of Jan. 7, when Gretzky scored three goals as the Oilers beat the visiting Hartford Whalers 5–3 in Northlands Coliseum. Gretzky's hat trick – his 48th, 49th and 50th goals of the season – put him only three games off his 1981–82 record pace, when he scored 50 goals in 39 games, the achievement of which he is proudest. However, his league record of 17 consecutive games in which he had one or more assists came to an end that night, despite his assisting on one goal by his mere presence on the ice and without ever touching the puck. Linemate Jaroslav Pouzar, out on the ice to do Gretzky's backchecking for him, was carrying the puck. Gretzky was on Pouzar's left, and Hartford defenseman Risto Siltanen was backing up, nervously glancing at and leaning toward Gretzky. When Pouzar faked a pass to Gretzky, Siltanen bought the whole act, rushing over to grab Gretzky, only to watch helplessly while Pouzar scored on a clear shot for a 2–0 Edmonton lead.

After scoring an empty-net goal in the final minute, Gretzky faced the standard postgame media crush while Barnett and Gretzky's investments counselor, Ian Barrigan, waited to talk over some business. They are two members of the four-man team (the others are Gretzky's agent, Gus Badali, and father, Walter) that handles Gretzky's business affairs. He reportedly makes $1 million a year for playing hockey and more than twice that in endorsements and investments.

Gretzky currently endorses nine products, including Mattel games. Titan hockey sticks and a new General Mills cereal, Pro Stars, which has his picture on the box. Gretzky maintains an office at CorpSport headquarters, about a block from his apartment. He goes there once or twice a week to tackle a desk heaped with paperwork. Barnett sorts it into "sign only," "read and discuss," "read only" and "Wayne – personal" piles. The more than 5,000 pieces of fan mail he gets each month are answered by a staff headed by Sophie Moss, the mother of his girl friend, Canadian pop singer Vickie Moss.

"The businessman in Wayne is emerging," says Barnett. "Two years ago he'd look at a contract and ask, 'How much money?' Last year it was 'How much time?' Now it's 'What's the small print and the full potential?'"

"Every shift I take is one shift closer to the last one," says Gretzky. "When my career is over I want to be financially set so I can do whatever I want." Then he smiles. "Of course, I have no idea what that will be."

For now, Gretzky's goal is to stay at the peak of his game "for eight, nine, 10 years. I admire guys like Marcel Dionne and Mike Bossy. They get their points every year." Gretzky attributes his performance this season – thus far his finest – to fear and, as a result, better mental preparation.

"I knew I left myself open to criticism by going to Hollywood and doing all the things I did this summer," he said the other day on a flight to Detroit. "If I didn't have a good year people would think hockey wasn't my top priority anymore. All summer I kept telling myself, 'This has to be my year.' Physically, I don't do much. Maybe a little running and tennis...." Gretzky stopped talking and leaned forward as the plane encountered some turbulence. He grabbed the back of the seat in front of him with his left hand, bent over and stared at the floor. "Wait a minute. Just a minute. It's bumpy...I hate flying."

While Gretzky says his dislike of air travel would never induce him to quit hockey, others say the fear is getting worse; other things being equal, it may one day be a factor in a decision to retire. Until then it's hypnosis (which worked only temporarily) and Dramamine (which keeps him from throwing up).

Though he looked tired, almost haggard, on the bus ride to Joe Louis Arena, Gretzky seemed to glow once he was on the ice for the evening's practice. He flew through routine drills until Sather, who doesn't want to see his star burn himself out in practice, chased him off the ice. Gretzky plays 26 to 28 minutes per game skating a regular shift, killing penalties and working the power plays.

Acknowledging his increasing maturity. Sather made Gretzky team captain this season, and he's very much a team leader. In the dressing room his joy seemed contagious as he boogied a couple of dance steps with a naked Mark Messier, who was en route to the shower, and then smiled steadily while team public relations director Bill Tuele read out loud a letter sent Express Mail to Gretzky from a girl in New Jersey. She wanted to fix up Gretzky with her girl friend, "who has a real knockout hairdo" but who has been a little down on her luck lately, what with "really getting leveled by a Chevy truck."

"Hey, I knew a girl in high school who looked like she'd been hit by a Chevy," said Gretzky.

He seemed genuinely loose.

A column in the next day's *Detroit Free Press* compared Gretzky's then 42-game streak to the 44-game streaks of Pete Rose and Willie Keeler. Last stops before DiMaggio.

That night, before 19,557, the streak continued, beginning with a remarkable shorthanded goal. With the precision of a pickpocket, Gretzky kicked the puck off the stick of Detroit rookie Steve Yzerman and onto his own stick. Then he wheeled in front of the net, pulling goalie Greg Stefan (his boyhood friend and Pee Wee teammate) off the near post. Gretzky put a low shot into the small opening left by Stefan on the short side. The goal gave Edmonton a 4–0 first-period lead and moved Gretzky to within one goal of Dionne's record of 10 shorthanded goals in one season.

Walter Gretzky, a straightforward, wholly unpretentious man who had driven to the game from the family home in Brantford, Ont., walked into the arena minutes after the goal. After hearing a description of it he said, "Wayne used his feet well. That's something most hockey players can't do. And he has the timing to strip a guy of the puck. He's on them before they know it."

In the second period the crowd reacted with a sort of collective murmur each time Gretzky touched the puck. Walter Gretzky shook his head. "How'd you like to live like that?" he said. "People expecting a miracle every time you step on the ice. That's pressure."

A superb goal, if not quite a miracle, was served up at 13:42 of the second period after Gretzky stole the puck from Detroit defenseman Greg Smith. He lifted Smith's stick, snaked the puck away and snapped a 25-footer just over Stefan's glove and under the crossbar. It was a pretty, if not high-percentage, shot, but as Gretzky said after the game, "One hundred percent of the shots you don't take don't go in."

Twenty-nine seconds after his second goal, Gretzky passed to Willy Lindstrom for another score. "Gretzky doesn't just make a good pass," said Lindstrom later, "he makes the perfect pass."

"That's two points this shift, Walter," yelled Murray Angus, a friend of the Gretzkys, slapping Walter on the shoulder. The older Gretzky neither cheered nor smiled. "Poor Greg," he said, referring to Stefan, "I drove to the game with his father. Wayne never had a bigger booster than Frank Stefan."

Loyalty like that apparently runs in the family, and it recently got the younger Gretzky in trouble. After the Oilers bombed the New Jersey Devils 13–4 in Edmonton Nov. 19, an angry Gretzky, who should have been elated with his eight points in the game, said, "They [the Devils] are putting a Mickey Mouse operation on the ice. They had better start getting better personnel. It's ruining hockey."

The next day Gretzky issued an apology. "I wish I hadn't said it," he admits now, "but their starting goalie that night, Ronnie Low, is a good friend of mine. I felt badly for him."

On Jan. 11, two days after the Detroit game, the Oilers played the Black Hawks in Chicago, and the streak hype was building, GRETZKY RUNS OUT OF GOALS - JOE DIMAGGIO'S STREAK ONLY REMAINING TARGET read a headline in the *Chicago Tribune*.

That night the Oilers jumped to a 4–1 second-period lead, but thus far Gretzky had no points. He was being well checked by Chicago center Troy Murray, whose strategy is to stay in front of Gretzky, impeding his progress. It was 4–2 with 3:22 to play, Gretzky still zip, when Chicago defenseman Dave Feamster scored to make it 4–3.

"They'll be pulling the goalie," said Oiler assistant coach Ted Green.

In the past 10 minutes, Gretzky, his disclaimers about the pressure of the streak notwithstanding, had been sneaking glances at the clock. With 32 seconds to play, Chicago goalie Tony Esposito, who had robbed Gretzky with a glove save on a first-period breakaway, left the game in favor of an extra attacker. As the Black Hawks swarmed around the Oiler goal, Gretzky was high in the slot, covering the Chicago point men and waiting for a chance.

The puck finally left the Oilers zone, and with seven seconds to go, Gretzky made a play of, well, Gretzkyan proportions. His nemesis, Murray, retrieved the puck in neutral ice and tried to flip it past Gretzky to Hawk defenseman Doug Wilson. Gretzky flicked the puck with his stick, and it bounced high. He reached up, batted it to the ice with his left glove, used his body to shield the puck from the desperately back-checking Murray, and skated over the blue line toward the empty Chicago goal. From 25 feet he slid the puck into the cage.

Hello, Pete Rose and Willie Keeler. Beer cups rained down from the balcony, littering the ice. Chicago fans, once among the best in the league, began their puerile chant: "Gretzky sucks. Gretzky sucks." Amid the din and the garbage, Wayne Gretzky was hugging his teammates, a huge smile softening the sharpness of his face.

In DiMaggio's world that goal would have been a legged-out single on an 0–2 pitch in the bottom of the ninth.

"Wayne uses the pressure," says Sather. "He converts it to energy and channels it into his game."

On Friday night in Buffalo Gretzky handled the pressure better than did his Oiler teammates by assisting on Pat Hughes's goal at 7:11 of the third period, his only point in a 3–1 Oiler loss.

"The best thing about the streak." Gretzky said earlier in the week, "is that it's good for hockey. The game needs the attention."

But on Sunday in New Jersey, it seemed as though some of the fun had gone out of the streak when Gretzky admitted, "The pressure to get a point every night is beginning to bother me a little." Apparently very little. Despite the potential distraction of seeing Devil fans wearing Mickey Mouse headgear and carrying signs, one of which said, in part, GRETZKY IS GOOFY (apologies apparently cut no ice in New Jersey), the leader of the NHL scoring club stuck it in their mouse ears with three assists in a 5–4 Edmonton win.

On Monday morning Gretzky and the Oilers headed home to Edmonton, the streak intact at 46. As his remarkable run continued, regardless of the validity of its comparison with DiMaggio's, Gretzky was reaffirming the fact that he is the genius of his sport and, like DiMaggio, a hero to turn one's lonely eyes to.

Gretzky's point steak lasted five more games, ending at 51. During the streak, he collected 153 points, an average of exactly three points a game.

THE KEY MAN IS SHARPER

BY JACK FALLA | FEBRUARY 18, 1985

In his sixth NHL season, the Oilers' Wayne Gretzky was better than ever, but he still didn't think he'd reached his best

(Photograph by Heinz Kluetmeier)

THE PRIME OF WAYNE GRETZKY IS CLOSE UPON US.
The man is maturing, and the player is at or near his peak. But even as Gretzky reaffirms himself this season as the best scorer in hockey history, his stats have begun to lose their ability to amaze – so many of the records he breaks are his own, anyway – leaving us to focus less on the unprecedented heights he has reached than on the artistry of his attainment, the changes in his life and his game, and the unflagging joy that sustains him.

But first the numbers. With the season slightly more than half over, Gretzky has already made a shambles of the NHL scoring race. At the All-Star break, he led the league in goals, with 54, and assists, with 99 – two goals and 49 points more than his Edmonton Oiler linemate Jari Kurri, who was in second place in both categories – en route to what will be his fifth consecutive scoring title. At his current pace of 2.73 points a game, Gretzky will finish the season with a record 218 points, breaking his own NHL record of 212 set in 1981–82. Barring injury or slump, he's a lock to win a record sixth consecutive Hart Trophy as the league's MVP.

Gretzky's scoring pace has been so fast that this season he became the youngest player – he was 24 on Jan. 26 – to reach two significant career milestones. On Dec. 19 he became only the 18th player in NHL history to reach the 1,000-point plateau (Bryan Trottier of the Islanders became the 19th on Jan. 29), accomplishing in 5½ seasons what took the other 18 an average of 16 seasons. The second fastest among them, Guy Lafleur, required nine seasons. And on Jan. 13 Gretzky scored his 400th NHL goal, reaching that level 70 games earlier than Mike Bossy, who previously had been the fastest man to 400. At his league-record career average of .915 goals a game, Gretzky will finish this season in 16th place on the alltime scoring list and will surpass his boyhood hero, Gordie Howe (801), as the NHL's leading career goal scorer late in the 1989–90 season, accomplishing in 11 years what Howe took 26 to do.

But while Gretzky rockets past milestones as though they were slats in a picket fence, there are other, more subtle, changes in his game and his life. The Kid is growing up.

"Birthdays," says Glen Sather, Edmonton's coach and general manager. "That's the biggest change in this whole team. Wayne is maturing. I don't know if he's at his peak, but he's as good as he ever was."

"I think he's going to have one big, *big* year," says assistant coach John Muckler, "maybe when he's around 27 or 28."

A 300-point year?

"Sounds impossible in an 80-game season, but if anybody can do it, that kid can," says Muckler.

"Physically, I may be at my peak now," says Gretzky, "but, with what I'm learning, I think it might be sometime in the next couple or three years that I'll be playing my best."

One thing he has learned is to cut down on taking theatrical dives and yapping at officials, for years major offenses on the Gretzky rap sheet. With the score 3–3 in the third period of a Jan. 16 game against the New York Islanders, Gretzky broke down the right wing on a good scoring chance, only to be hooked down by Islander defenseman Denis Potvin. There was no call. The crowd screamed for a penalty, and Gretzky, who in past years would have turned this one into a case of vintage whine – exaggerating his fall, lying on the ice a few extra seconds, imploring the referee for justice – instead bounced up, said nothing and got back into the play. This pattern has been repeated all season.

"He didn't enjoy having the reputation of a guy who whines, so he's taking his shots and playing tougher," says Dave Semenko, once Gretzky's left wing/bodyguard, and now a player who's rarely on the ice with the Great One.

Los Angeles Kings coach Pat Quinn says, "He still draws close coverage, but he's learned to deal with it on a different emotional level."

Exactly. "The big thing with me is that I play emotionally," says Gretzky. "I used to let the emotion run away with me. If I got fouled, I'd blame the ref or the other player. Now my attitude is, if the ref calls it, fine; if not, I'm not going to change his mind."

One prevailing misconception about Gretzky and the Oilers is that he and they can't, or won't, play defense. He can, and they will. While Gretzky isn't one to make diving blocks of shots, he back-checks better than the critics say. With 28 seconds to play in the second period of that Islander game, with Edmonton leading 3–2, New York's Greg Gilbert broke away on the left wing. Gretzky, coming all the way from the opposite wing, caught Gilbert at the top of the face-off circle and swiped the puck before he could shoot.

"This season we'll come into the dressing room leading 5–0 after two periods, and Wayne will say, 'Never mind winning 10–5, let's go for the shutout,'" says Oiler defenseman Kevin Lowe.

But the Oilers can still chalk it up and run the table when they have to. In an 8–7 win over Los Angeles on Jan. 21, Edmonton produced six unanswered goals – Gretzky scored one and set up the game winner – in 18:40 to overcome a 7–2 deficit.

As always, Gretzky's artistry is in his offense. A four-game stretch in January offered a sampler of his virtuosity. In the game with the Islanders, Gretzky the Sniper scored on a slap shot, short side, from the top of the left circle. Two nights later, in a 4–4 tie at Vancouver, Gretzky the Opportunist saw a puck bounce out of goalie Richard Brodeur's glove and bunted it into the net while it was three feet off the ice. The next night against the Canucks in Edmonton, Gretzky the Magician banked one in from behind the net off Brodeur's left skate in a 7–5 win. And two nights later against L.A., Gretzky the Technician moved through heavy traffic to the right of the Kings' goal and, maneuvering rookie defenseman Craig Redmond as a screen, scored on a shot off the left post.

To watch Gretzky is a pleasure, but to skate with him is a privilege and a revelation for a guy like me, who still plays pickup hockey on a regular basis. The ice in Northlands Coliseum is still smooth with the morning resurfacing when Sather starts the first of the warmup line rushes in an Oiler practice session. I don't take the first run with Gretzky; instead I go with Mark Messier and Gord Sherven, and I'm already well behind the play at the red line, where the dominant sensation is hearing Messier's skates ripping the ice...*scrunch...scrunch...scrunch* under the pressure of his tremendous leg drive. A few minutes later, as I skate with Gretzky and Sather, it's different. The speed is the same – almost incomprehensible to this average skater – but Gretzky seems to be moving lightly, his skates barely cutting the ice with a *snick...snick...snick*. The pass from Gretzky to me is perfect, soft and on the stick blade, and my only thought is to get it back to him before he's out of range. But my return pass is terrible, in his skates on his backhand side. In virtually one motion he flicks the puck off his right skate onto his stick and snaps a shot between the goalie's legs. On the rush back, Kurri leaves a drop pass for me in the slot, but it seems somehow presumptuous to shoot, so I pass quickly to Gretzky. He passes it back immediately. I give it to him again at the crease – he has to shoot now – and begin gliding around the net. Incredibly, Gretzky centers the puck from behind the goal line past the goalie and across the crease to me for an easy tap-in. He smiles and yells as the puck clanks against the back of the cage. The look on his face is the same one I've seen on children in backyard rinks. "He still loves the game," says Sather, "and he shows up every day."

There are many manifestations of Gretzky's love of the game. Gretzky says, on the last page of *Gretzky*, the book his father, Walter, wrote with Jim Taylor, "...maybe it's just as well that I live in a penthouse. If I lived at street level in Edmonton, the winter would come and I'd look out the window at the kids playing road hockey, and before you know it I'd be out there with them and there would go my game that night."

The view from Gretzky's duplex penthouse on Super Bowl Sunday is of the frozen North Saskatchewan River and the west side of Edmonton. Inside, on the 18th-floor level, Gretzky is sprawled on the couch in front of his over-sized TV screen, watching the game in the company of teammates Sherven (since traded to Minnesota) and Marc Habscheid, two bachelors called up from Edmonton's Halifax farm club only weeks before, and Jim and Joey Moss, brothers of Gretzky's girl friend, Vickie Moss.

"Oh, what an offense," says Gretzky as Dan Marino leads Miami to a short-lived 10–7 lead. Gretzky may have a newfound respect for defense, but he has a deep-rooted faith in offense.

Vickie enters the room. She and Gretzky have been together for six years, and they are obviously comfortable with each other. Easy. Settled.

"Who are you rooting for, Wayne Gretzky?" she asks.

"Miami. Who are you for, Moss?"

"Ah...the team that has Joe Marino."

Everyone laughs. Gretzky is beside himself. "Oh, Moss, you sportaholic," he says, throwing his head back on the couch.

She laughs.

"We've talked about marriage, but not a whole lot," says Gretzky later. "Right now we'd like to get Vickie settled in her career."

Moss is a pop singer who expects to record a demo soon for Canadian-born producer David Foster, who works with Kenny Rogers and Chicago. He's a hockey fan whom she met when Gretzky took him to hear her sing.

After dinner she plays a tape of a song she recently recorded. The vocal is full and clear: "Baby, you can save my life...."

Throughout the Super Bowl, Gretzky has been taking phone calls, some concerning his planned purchase of a Junior A team, probably the Hull (Que.) Olympiques. "You've got to have some fun with your money," he says, though he adds, "I'm usually a low-risk guy. I'm happy to turn $100,000 into $150,000 instead of trying to turn it into $4 million."

Gretzky estimates he has seven to 10 more years in the NHL, and he rules out the possibility of staying in the game as a coach or G.M. "What I do is instinctive," he says. "I feel my way down the ice. I see where I want to go, and I go there. How could I coach that?" But he can see himself as an owner.

In the meantime, he's perhaps doubling his $1 million-a-year playing income – his contract with Oiler owner Peter Pocklington extends through 1999 – with endorsements and the commercials he does for Travelers Insurance, Canon cameras, Titan hockey sticks, Nike sportswear, William Neilson Ltd., a chocolate company, Mattel toys and his own General Mills cereal, Pro Stars. It's no wonder he has all those sources of outside income, because he's undoubtedly the most recognizable and well-liked hockey player in history. A study of public recognition and popularity in the U.S. of 110 sports personalities was made last April by Marketing Evaluations/TvQ. In it, Gretzky ranked only slightly below the average for all athletes in familiarity, 37% vs. 44%, which is astonishing considering that hockey is popular mainly in the Northern states. And he's well above the average in Q rating (a measure of how well he is liked by those familiar with him), with a score of 23, compared with the average of 14.

But what's not to like?

Besides making corporate pitches, Gretzky is a spokesman for several charities, including the Canadian Association for the Mentally Retarded, for which he and Joey Moss have just completed a national television spot. Joey, 22, a victim of Down's syndrome, works as the Oilers' clubhouse boy, a job Gretzky helped him get, but which he keeps on his own.

"Wayne really loves Joey," says Habscheid. "If anyone ever did anything to Joey, Wayne would go crazy." The relationship lends credence to Gretzky's assertion that he looks forward to someday "getting married and having kids."

He also looks forward, according to Lowe, "not just to breaking more records but to someday taking his place with the almighties, the immortals – the Howes, the Béliveaus, the guys who led their teams to repeat Stanley Cups."

The Great Gretzky is very much with us, but the Kid is a kid no longer.

Gretzky never made it to 300 points in a season. During the 1984–85 season, he reached 208, and the next year he bested his previous record of 212 points by three, an NHL record considered all but untouchable.

HOT SHOTS ON ICE

BY AUSTIN MURPHY | JUNE 1, 1987

Wayne Gretzky and the Oilers were ready to reclaim the Stanley Cup after a scorching performance against the Flyers

(Photograph by Bruce Bennett/Getty Images)

WE SHOULD ALL BE SO FORTUNATE TO SLUMP THE WAY Wayne Gretzky slumps. When the Edmonton Oilers' number 99 went without a goal in five straight Stanley Cup playoff games, his scoring drought took on the tenor of a national emergency in Western Canada. Newspapers ran big headlines: WHAT'S WRONG WITH WAYNE? Maybe he hadn't recovered from the mugging Dale Hawerchuk had given him during the Winnipeg series. The talk shows rang with speculation that the 26-year-old Gretzky had lost it. Why, he hadn't won a new automobile in almost a week. Indeed about the only unconcerned man in town seemed to be Oiler president/G.M./coach Glen Sather.

"I laugh when people say something's wrong with Wayne," Sather said. "Personally I've never seen him have a bad game. A lot of nights he's a decoy, opening things for the other guys. And over the last five weeks, we've asked him to do a lot more defensively. Slump? He's been great!"

On Sunday night in Philadelphia, Gretzky was ethereal against the Flyers as Edmonton scored a solid 4–1 victory to take a three-games-to-one lead in the Stanley Cup finals. The Great One's play shone with the glow he takes on when everything's working and he's seven steps ahead of everyone else. After Jari Kurri, Kevin Lowe and Randy Gregg each scored off pinpoint passes from Gretzky, both locker rooms paid tribute to the man who has been named the NHL's Most Valuable Player for a record seven straight seasons. "There will never be another player like him," said teammate Kent Nilsson. "He dominated," said Flyer goaltender Ron Hextall.

"I had it pretty good tonight," Gretzky admitted. "I don't know what happens or when it happens...the night before the game, the morning of it. Sometimes it takes a hard hit on your first shift to get your head in the game. I felt confident tonight. I wanted the puck."

And then Gretzky took his puck back home to Edmonton, where the Oilers hoped to wrap up their third Cup championship in four years on Tuesday night.

When it started, the Cup final seemed to have something for everyone. The freewheeling and speedy Oilers against the steady, grind-it-out (or goon-it-up) Flyers. North Americans from Beaverlodge, Alberta, to Marcus Hook, Pa., could sit back and enjoy. That pleased the TV folks. Moreover, the series pitted the NHL's two best regular-season teams. That made the league happy. The final was vindication, as the NHL saw it, of its profitable, protracted and decidedly unpopular playoff format. Even the weather cooperated: Six inches of snow fell on Edmonton one day last week, making it easy to forget that the baseball season was almost two months old. To top it all off, the final featured the sport's most scintillating player, slump or no slump.

In Game 1, Philadelphia mistakenly tried to skate with the much faster Oilers. Catastrophe struck early in the third period when Glenn Anderson, Paul Coffey and Jari Kurri scored three unanswered goals in nine minutes to give Edmonton a 4–2 win. Cured of any delusions about team speed, the Flyers returned to their roots for Game 2: They hit hard, finished their checks and scored when they had good chances. And Flyer coach Mike Keenan had the needle out for Gretzky. At one point he stood on his bench to give Gretzky a tongue-lashing. "We had a verbal exchange," said Keenan, who objected to Gretzky's "taking dives." Keenan's concern, as he later explained it, was not so much that the referee might be influenced by one of Gretzky's alleged snow jobs but that the long-term welfare of the game would suffer. "It's poor conduct," lectured Keenan. "You expect more from the best hockey player in the world. All he's doing is embarrassing the officials, and this is the second game in a row he's done that."

Gretzky later said that he hadn't heard Keenan, and he laughed at his allegations. "When you're 160 [pounds] and you get hooked," said Gretzky, "you generally go down."

Much to Keenan's chagrin, Gretzky was clearly upright when he scored a tap-in goal off a perfect pass from Kurri to give the Oilers a 1–0 lead. But the Flyers rallied for a 2–1 lead after two periods and had reason to feel a bit smug. Fifty times this season they had taken leads into the third period, and only once had they lost the game.

Make that twice. Anderson's spectacular game-tying goal illustrated the difference between these teams. Gathering in Gregg's long, cross-ice pass, Anderson burst through two dark jerseys at the blue line. Doug Crossman, the Flyers' last line of defense, tried to ride him off the puck, but Anderson hopped left, tucked the puck beneath Crossman's stick, windmilling his own stick over Crossman's head, met the puck on the other side of Crossman and slid it past Hextall – a goal for the 11 o'clock news. "Along the ice, stick side – that's the best shot in hockey," said Anderson. "I'll use that one once in a blue moon. Maybe when I'm playing on the pond."

Whatever, it was the type of goal that Edmonton seems to score with regularity and Philadelphia can only dream about – or see on the Oilers' highlight film.

The ensuing overtime was history as soon as Gretzky crossed the Flyer blue line, pulled up and began stick-handling, daring the Flyers to converge. Holding the puck, holding it longer – Gretzky possesses what has been described as the highest "panic point" in the game – rattling the Flyers with his calm, the Great One found Coffey open on the point. Coffey faked a slap shot and, with bodies hurtling toward him, tapped the puck to the uncovered Kurri, who one-timed it past Hextall on the short side. Ticktacktoe, three men in a row, 3–2.

The Flyers had turned in two strong performances but trailed in the series two games to none. "We're running out of adjustments," said forward Rick Tocchet. And even though the Flyers were traveling home to the raucous confines of the Spectrum, their demise was taking on a not-if-but-when inevitability.

The Spectrum lends literal meaning to the expression "home-ice advantage," with an ice surface reputed to be the NHL's worst, more easily gouged and more quickly rutted than any other in the league. "Put on my skates and see for yourself," says Philly defenseman Brad Marsh. Rough ice, of course, is better suited for a grind-it-out bunch than for a team of fancy-footed artistes.

Adding to the home advantage for Game 3 Friday night was a macabre pregame rite concocted by Flyer officials. The Spectrum was plunged into complete darkness, save for cones of hard white light that focused on players while they were introduced. Then the vision of Kate Smith appeared on the giant video screen. As the late songstress belted out *God Bless America*, all good Flyer fans sang along: *"...to dee oceans, white wit' foam...."* The Flyers had a 56–9–2 record in games that followed Ms. Smith's rendition, and did they ever need her now.

Twenty-two minutes into Game 3, the drama appeared to be over. Though the Flyers had played valiantly, they trailed 3–0. Worse, Anderson had just scored his 13th goal of the playoffs without taking a shot. "He came in, tried to go to his left and missed the puck," said Hextall, shaking his head. "It fooled both of us." Anderson's nonshot crawled between Hextall's pads, and Flyer fans, deafening from the opening face-off, went mute. You could hear the vendors across the rink hawking their soft pretzels.

Then, as Sather observed, "The water started to tip out of the bucket." Sitting comfortably on their fat lead, the Oilers let the Flyers back into the game. Center Murray Craven, making only his second appearance since breaking his left foot in April, swept an off-speed backhander past goal-tender Grant Fuhr: 3–1. Peter Zezel's pass across the crease caromed off Craig Muni and skidded over the line: 3–2. Scott Mellanby's blast grazed Fuhr's pads and found the back of the net: 3–3. Brad McCrimmon deflected Mellanby's pass for a score: 4–3. Brian Propp drove home a 90-footer into an empty net: 5–3. It was a Flyer comeback for the ages.

The startling turn of events was not well received by Sather. "That first goal was created by a very borderline penalty call," he said. Craven had scored on a power play after linesman Kevin Collins called the Oilers for too many men on the ice. "I guess Collins just wanted to have his name in the paper," said Sather, who perhaps had forgotten that a holding call with no time left in the first period of Game 2 had provided Edmonton a two-man advantage – and a goal.

On Sunday night, tensions boiled over in the pregame warmups – sound familiar? – when Edmonton's Kevin Lowe shot a puck in Hextall's direction. "To tell the truth, I thought it was [backup goalie] Chico Resch," said Lowe. "I guess Ron thought I was trying to disrupt him." Both teams massed troops at the red line. Skirmishes broke out, but nothing serious erupted.

And then it was the Great Gretzky show. First he set up Kurri in the slot: 1–0. Next he lured two Flyers away from Hextall and fed a goalmouth pass to Lowe for an easy score: 2–0. After the Flyers cut the Oilers' lead to 2–1 on a goal by McCrimmon, Gretzky found Gregg in the slot and Hextall was beat again: 3–1. Mike Krushelnyski put the Flyers to rest with a third-period breakaway goal for the final 4–1 margin. Unfortunately Hextall then tried to take out his frustrations on perhaps the most timid player on the ice, Oiler forward Kent Nilsson. As Nilsson skated past the Flyer net, Hextall grabbed his stick in both hands and gave the Swede a vicious chop behind the right knee that left him crumpled on the ice in pain.

"If that had been Mike Schmidt, it would have been out of the park," Nilsson said after the game, an ice pack strapped to his leg. Nilsson's complaint? "When goaltenders do it, they don't serve their penalty. They stay in the net. He got 15 minutes and never left the ice!"

This night, however, belonged to Gretzky and the Oilers. As the last seconds ticked off the clock, fans in the Spectrum rose to applaud the defeated Flyers. It was as if they didn't expect to see them again this season.

The Flyers would recover, albeit temporarily. Philadelphia won the next game in Edmonton 4–3. The Oilers again failed to clinch in Game 6, a 3–2 loss at the Spectrum. Game 7 was won when Jari Kurri scored the game-winner in front of a home crowd off a Gretzky pass.

HERE'S THAT MAN AGAIN

BY AUSTIN MURPHY | MAY 2, 1988

After a quiet (for him) regular season, Wayne Gretzky had
Edmonton flying in the Stanley Cup playoffs

(Photograph by Bruce Bennett/Getty Images)

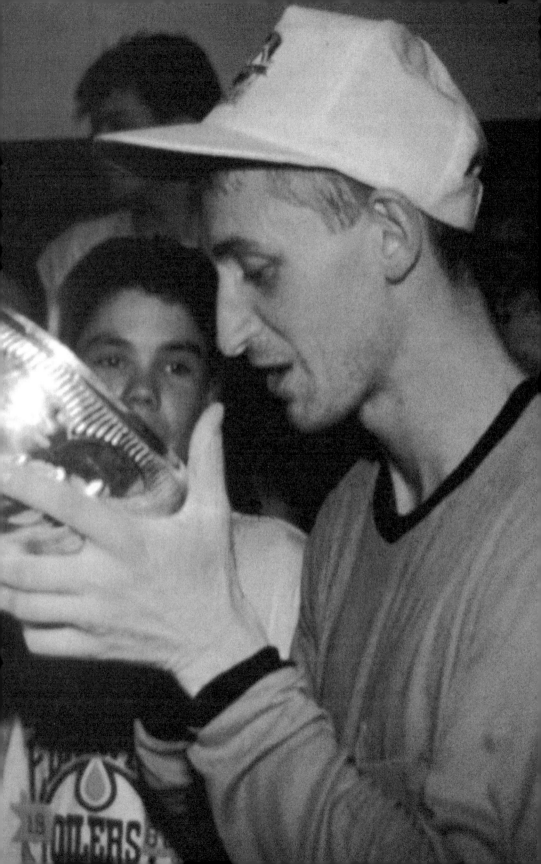

FOR A DYNASTY-IN-THE-OFFING, IT HAD BEEN A DISQUIETING, indeed, a humbling season for the Edmonton Oilers. Wayne Gretzky lost the scoring title that had been his for seven years, and, suddenly, the Oilers – missing half a dozen stars from last year's dream team – weren't even the best club in the Smythe Division. That honor went to the up-and-coming Calgary Flames, who had the NHL's best regular-season record. Long oppressed by Edmonton, their hostile intra-Alberta neighbor to the north, the Flames were hungry. They had depth. They had momentum. And now the Flames, unceremoniously swept from the Stanley Cup playoffs in four games by the Oilers, have learned the hard way that all-world players like Gretzky, Mark Messier, Jari Kurri, Glenn Anderson and Grant Fuhr tend to offset those little difficulties. And like the Montreal Canadiens, Calgary now knows that come April, regular-season standings have a way of fading into irrelevance.

Montreal had the next-best record behind Calgary, but they trailed the Boston Bruins three games to one, having scored but one goal in two games at Boston Garden. The Bruins appeared to be coping successfully with the ghosts of ugly playoff performances past.

Amid all the combat, it was the NHL's efforts to tidy its image that took it on the chin. Indeed, it was fortunate for Edmonton's Marty McSorley, for the Oilers and for the league that Edmonton won Game 3 by more than a single goal (4–2), because the Oilers' second goal, which was allowed to stand, stank to high heaven. Midway through the second period with the score tied 1–1, McSorley was walloped hard into the boards by Gary Roberts. He got up groggily, all the while grousing to referee Andy van Hellemond that a penalty should have been called. In fact, the check was clean, if painful – precisely the kind of check by which the minimally skilled McSorley has earned his livelihood for four NHL seasons. Van Hellemond properly ignored him and followed play up the ice. Skating toward his bench, McSorley speared the first red jersey he saw, that of Mike Bullard, a former teammate on the Pittsburgh Penguins. McSorley jammed his stick into Bullard's lower abdomen with such force that the blade snapped. Bullard crumpled to the ice and lay motionless. Meanwhile, before linesman Gord Broseker, who had seen the spear, could whistle the play dead, Oiler Charlie Huddy's slap shot from the point eluded Flames goaltender Mike Vernon and made the score 2–1. Bullard was subsequently taken off the ice on a stretcher.

Although McSorley, who should be suspended for his cold-blooded assault, was assessed a five-minute major and a game misconduct and was ejected from the game, Huddy's goal stood. Calgary assistant general manager Al MacNeil later labeled the ref "Andy Van Solomon. I guess you could call that splitting the baby in half. He gave them something [the goal], and he gave us something [the power play]. They got the gold mine, we got the shaft."

Still, the Flames managed to undermine themselves, failing to score then and seven other times they were a man up. As throughout the series, Calgary's uncharacteristically limp power play – during the regular season it had been the NHL's best – did more to demoralize the team than to help it. "We're living on borrowed time," Calgary coach Terry Crisp said after Saturday's game.

McSorley's pitchfork aside, the Oilers, who have been quietly reminding people all season that Lord Stanley's Cup still belongs to Edmonton, must now be considered the Cup favorites. The Oilers defensemen, as disciplined as Gretzky & Co. were dazzling, stonewalled the Flames' big guns: Hakan Loob, Joe Nieuwendyk, Joey Mullen and Bullard.

Gretzky played like a superstar with a chip on his shoulder. The Great One had missed 16 regular-season games because of injuries and, consequently, had yielded the scoring title to Pittsburgh's Mario Lemieux. Ever gracious, Gretzky frequently congratulated Lemieux. But there was always an edge to his voice. Says Oilers coach Glen Sather, "Wayne is very proud, very aware of everything he's accomplished. Believe me, he's not about to give anything away." The Flames will concur.

Did the Oilers respect Calgary? Gretzky, who does not make such statements lightly, called his team's 3–1 win in Game 1, which he sealed with a breakaway goal late in the game, "the biggest in team history." Twice in Game 2 the Oilers found themselves trailing by two goals; twice they came back. Kurri, sensational in the playoffs after a disappointing season, waltzed around Flames defenseman Paul Reinhart and beat Vernon with a low, 25-foot slap with four minutes left in regulation, tying the game 4–4. Then, with his team short-handed in overtime, Gretzky took a long outlet pass from Kurri at center ice, swooped down on Vernon and, at a nearly impossible angle, rocketed the puck into the far left corner of the net.

"Maybe getting hurt was a blessing in disguise," said Gretzky. "Not just for this year, but for my whole career. I've played a lot of hockey over the last 10 years, Canada Cups, All-Star games, exhibition games, playoff games. This year I missed a good six weeks. The more Slats [Sather] played me tonight, the better I felt."

This series had seemed the likeliest of the NHL's four divisional finals to go seven games, which made the Flames' failure to win at home all the more shocking. With Boston dominating Montreal – after losing all 18 of its postseason series with the Habs since 1943 – and New Jersey, the worst team in the NHL last season, two wins from the Patrick Division championship after splitting four games with Washington, it appeared this season's quota of playoff miracles had been filled. In the Norris Division, the favored Detroit Red Wings led St. Louis three games to one.

Boston got a rude reception on April 18, the night the Adams Division finals began, when an ice storm damaged a transmission line in northern Quebec, plunging most of the province into darkness. Emergency generators helped light the Montreal Forum, enabling Game 1 between the Canadiens and Bruins to continue uninterrupted. "It was a good thing the game was blacked out [on TV], because we stunk out the joint," said Bruins center Bob Sweeney.

Early the next morning the power came back, as did the Bruins a day after that. Replacing Andy Moog, the loser in Game 1, goalie Rejean Lemelin stole Game 2 for the Bruins. Boston got off just 14 shots on goal but still won 4–3. "My glove was hot tonight," said Lemelin, 33, the Calgary reject whom the Bruins signed as a free agent last summer. In the first 10 minutes, Lemelin made three highlight-film saves on 50-goal scorer Stephane Richer. On Richer's fourth break-away the Forum crowd figured surely he would solve Lemelin this time. But Boston defenseman Michael Thelven took a two-handed chop that fractured Richer's right thumb and put him out for the series.

Vicious and premeditated, screamed the Habs.

"Vicious?" asked Thelven, a hardnosed, but hardly dirty, Swede. "Translation, please?"

"They should call them the Boston Villains," said Montreal coach Jean Perron, accusing the Bruins, who crashed Montreal defensemen Chris Chelios and Petr Svoboda into the boards all night, of using "goon tactics."

"He said that?" asked Boston's Ken (the Rat) Linseman. "What a bleeping hypocrite!"

Perron's coaching acumen notwithstanding, the Rat was right. Anybody who issues a uniform to the likes of John Kordic – who has zero hockey talent but a strong repertoire of jabs and uppercuts – leaves himself very little room for sanctimony.

Montreal sought retribution in Game 3 at Boston Garden. But while the Habs took runs at them, the Bruins took the game. Defenseman Ray Bourque was everywhere, throwing himself in front of shots and checking – cleanly – every Canadien in sight. Montreal was muffled as Lemelin was airtight again. The fact is, without Richer the Canadiens were just a bunch of grinders. The Bruins, on the other hand, were grinders with a mission, winning 3–1.

"They're playing like they think it's their year," said Perron, worriedly, before Game 4. His concern was well-founded. After 31 minutes of scoreless, breathless hockey, with Habs netminder Patrick Roy matching Lemelin save for save, Boston scored the only goal it would need. Bourque split Montreal's defense with a splendid breakout pass to Lyndon Byers, who found Middleton open on his left wing. Middleton, a former 51-goal scorer recently reduced to a bit part because of the presence of rookies Sweeney, Craig Janney and Bob Joyce, found his old touch, backhanding the puck over Roy's right leg pad for a 1–0 Bruins lead. Lemelin needed nothing more for Boston to win 2–0.

Lemelin has been the best goaltender in the playoffs – less spectacular than New Jersey prodigy Sean Burke, perhaps, but more consistent. The Devils, who flat out bullied the New York Islanders into submission in the first round, were themselves dominated by the Capitals in Game 1 of the Patrick Division finals. The Caps were sure they had arrived.

Maybe, but they didn't stay long. New Jersey won Games 2 and 3 by a combined score of 15–6. In Game 3, the teams danced their way to a playoff-record 62 penalties. Washington recovered to win Game 4 by a 4–1 score, but lost goalie Pete Peeters when he was hit on the mask, over his left eyebrow, by a John MacLean wrist shot. He suffered a concussion.

After his team was knocked out of the playoffs, Islanders general manager Bill Torrey was distressed because, as he put it, this year "someone is going to steal the Cup." Indeed, as a new week began, the Oilers, Bruins, Devils and Caps all had the look of thieves.

The Bruins and the Oilers would meet in the Stanley Cup finals in 1988, with Edmonton sweeping the series. Gretzky set a playoff record for assists (31) on his way to collecting his second Conn Smythe Trophy and fourth Stanley Cup.

WOE, CANADA

BY E.M. SWIFT | AUGUST 22, 1988

*A nation mourned as its hero was traded from Edmonton to
Los Angeles in a surprise move that changed hockey forever*
(Photograph by Bruce Bennett/Getty Images)

WAYNE GRETZKY, THE NEWEST MEMBER OF TINSELTOWN'S glitterati, was seated in the Polo Lounge of the Beverly Hills Hotel last Friday morning and speaking on the phone to his new boss, Bruce McNall, owner of the Los Angeles Kings. "*Who* called?" Gretzky asked McNall, a roly-poly 37-year-old who some 72 hours earlier had pulled off the unthinkable and put the historically hapless, inconsequential Kings onto the front pages of newspapers across North America. "You're kidding," said Gretzky. "Well how old is he? [*Pause*] Thirty-four? [*Pause*] Why not? What do you have to lose?"

Gretzky could not suppress a grin. At the end of a long – and at times grim – week, here was some news that tickled him. Guy Lafleur's agent had just contacted the team, saying that Lafleur, the former Montreal Canadiens great, wanted to come out of retirement and try out when the Kings' training camp opened in three weeks. So what if Lafleur is actually 36. The Great One skating side by side with the aging Flower in la-la land, which had suddenly become gaga land over hockey, was no less imaginable than the events that had transpired in the previous few days.

"I knew this thing would be big," Gretzky said, putting down the phone. "But I had no idea it would be this big."

In case you have been walking the picket lines outside *The Last Temptation of Christ* and have missed the news, on Aug. 9 the Kings and the Edmonton Oilers swung the biggest trade in NHL history and, at least monetarily, the biggest in the history of sports. In return for $15 million in cash, plus 20-year-old center Jimmy Carson, first-round draft picks in 1989, 1991 and 1993, and 18-year-old Martin Gelinas, who was the seventh player taken in the June draft, the Oilers traded Gretzky, now 27, who for the past nine years has been, to many, the Edmonton franchise, the spokesman for the game and the greatest hockey player in the world. In addition to Gretzky, the Oilers sent forward Mike Krushelnyski, 28, and tough-guy Marty McSorley, 25, to L.A. (The negotiating rights to a couple of unsigned defensemen – the Oilers' John Miner and the Kings' Craig Redmond – were also exchanged.) If the Great One's arrival in the City of Angels does not exactly mark the Second Coming, it's the closest thing to divine intervention that the Kings have seen in their 21 years of trying to put fannies in the seats of the Forum.

The deal stunned the sports world. Not since the Milwaukee Bucks sent Kareem Abdul-Jabbar to the Lakers in 1975 had an athlete of Gretzky's magnitude been traded in his prime. Because of the huge amount of money that changed hands, comparisons were immediately made to the 1919 deal which sent Babe Ruth from the Red Sox to the Yankees for $100,000. Reactions throughout the U.S. and Canada were immediate and wide-ranging:

- Canada's New Democratic Party House leader Nelson Riis: "Wayne Gretzky is a national symbol, like the beaver. How can we allow the sale of our national symbols? The Edmonton Oilers without Wayne Gretzky is like...*Wheel of Fortune* without Vanna White."
- Kings fan Earvin (Magic) Johnson: "Hey, he belongs in L.A. He's the greatest. I'm definitely going to get season tickets. Even if they never win a game, it will still be exciting to go now."
- Harry Sinden, Boston Bruin general manager: "It brings everyone in the league closer to Edmonton and brings Los Angeles closer to everyone."
- Pat Quinn, general manager of the Vancouver Canucks: "The Kings have got to try to be successful for the next three years, and if that doesn't work out they've left their team in mud for the next 10 to 15 years."
- Cliff Fletcher, general manager of the Calgary Flames: "All of a sudden the Kings have the potential to beat anybody in a short series. Gretzky won't tolerate anything less than winning."
- Brent Gretzky, 16-year-old brother of Wayne: "Los Angeles. That means I can fly to L.A. and check out the women."

Reaction in Edmonton, where the Oilers have won four of the last five Stanley Cups, was a bit more downbeat. "I feel like I did the day Elvis Presley died," one fan told *The Edmonton Sun*. Oiler owner Peter Pocklington's effigy was burned outside the Northlands Coliseum and city hall, and outraged citizens organized boycotts against two of Pocklington's companies, Gainer's meat packing and Palm

Dairies. Edmonton radio stations were inundated with calls from fans incorrectly blaming the trade on Gretzky's wife, U.S. actress Janet Jones, whom Gretzky married in an Edmonton wedding of royal style on July 16 and who is expecting the couple's first child around the New Year. Jones was called a "witch" and a "Jezebel," and newspapers across Canada quickly splashed racy headlines – 'JEZEBEL JANET!' – comparing her to Yoko Ono, who was blamed for breaking up the Beatles because of her relationship with John Lennon.

No one in Edmonton cared that Carson, the Southfield, Mich., native who was sent to the Oilers by the Kings, is seven years younger than Gretzky and scored 55 goals last year – only the second teenager, after Gretzky, to score more than 50 goals. No one wanted to hear about all those first-round draft choices, or about Gelinas, whom Fletcher calls "arguably the most talented player to come out of last year's draft."

Gretzky was a once-in-a-lifetime talent, brash on the ice and classy off it, the heart of a young, proud city stuck out in the middle of nowhere. It would be difficult to overstate what Gretzky – winner of eight of the last nine NHL Most Valuable Player awards, seven of the last eight scoring titles, holder of 41 individual NHL scoring records – meant to this remote prairie metropolis of 683,000 people. As *Sun* columnist Graham Hicks wrote: "He was our best reason for living here."

When the news of the deal first broke, Gretzky said that he had asked to be traded. The truth is he acquiesced to the idea and eventually forced the issue when he learned that Pocklington was shopping him around. Gretzky had signed a five-year contract with the Oilers in 1987; it paid him an annual salary of some $1.5 million. After June 15, 1992, Gretzky would be a free agent without compensation. Last February or March, according to Gretzky, Pocklington approached him and asked to renegotiate his contract so it would run for two more years. Gretzky, who has been saddled with long-term deals since he was 17, told him, "'Absolutely not.' I'd finally got my contract down to four years, and I didn't want to give that up."

The day after the Oilers won their fourth Stanley Cup, Gretzky learned from his agent, Mike Barnett, and his financial adviser, Ian Berrigan, that a group of Vancouver businessmen was trying to buy the Canucks and had offered Pocklington $22.5 million (Canadian) for Gretzky's services. Gretzky told his linemate Jari Kurri that he had a feeling he wouldn't be with the Oilers next season. "Unless I signed a new contract, which I wasn't willing to sign, I knew I was going to be traded." Gretzky says now.

In Pocklington's eyes, Gretzky – the third-leading scorer in NHL history, with career totals of 583 regular-season goals and a record 1,086 assists in just 696 games, the most exciting player in hockey, and the MVP of last spring's Stanley Cup playoffs – was a diminishing asset. Pocklington could command a Kings' ransom for Gretzky if he dealt him now. In four years, Gretzky could skip town for nothing.

In those intervening four years Gretzky might well have helped the Oilers win four more Stanley Cups and an even more commanding place in sports history. But hey, what's that compared with $15 million? Pocklington claims not to have needed the money. "All my companies are very healthy financially," he said last week. Still, in the early 1980s his financial empire, which currently includes real estate holdings, the meat packing plant, the dairy, the Oilers, the Edmonton Trappers (a Triple A baseball team), and the Edmonton Brick Men of the Canadian Soccer League, suffered a severe financial setback when the oil and real estate markets collapsed. He secured a loan using Gretzky's personal services contract with the Oilers as collateral, and reportedly still has some $67 million (Canadian) in loan arrangements with the Alberta government.

The Kings had been making overtures to Pocklington about Gretzky for the past two years. Jerry Buss had originally inquired, and after Buss sold the team last winter to McNall, his minority partner, the new owner reaffirmed his interest in Gretzky.

"A couple of days after Wayne's wedding he [Pocklington] called me and said, 'If you're serious about number 99, we should talk,'" McNall recalls. "He said that Jerry had originally offered him $15 million and any three players on the roster, and we used that as a starting point for the negotiations. I never did get him off that $15 million figure. The money issue was settled the fastest."

A self-made millionaire whose various enterprises include Numismatic Fine Arts, Inc., an ancient-coins business; Gladden Entertainment Corp., a motion picture company; and Sum-ma Stable. Inc., which races and breeds thoroughbreds, McNall reached Gretzky by phone at Jones's Sherman Oaks, Calif., apartment, six days into their honeymoon.

"You're kidding," said Gretzky when McNall explained that Pocklington had given him the O.K. to call.

Like most great athletes, Gretzky has tremendous pride which, when wounded, is slow to heal. It surprised and hurt him that Pocklington would not personally inform him that he was on the market. The hurt swiftly turned to anger. After his first conversation with McNall, Gretzky called his father, Walter, in Brantford, Ont. "My dad tried to get me to calm down," Gretzky says, "but I told him I'd already made up my mind I was never going to wear an Oilers' uniform again."

Any doubts about the move were dispelled after a phone call to Paul Coffey, his former Oiler teammate, who was traded last year to the Pittsburgh Penguins. "I asked Paul, 'Would you leave the Oilers if you had a chance to do it all over again?' It put him in a difficult position, since we won the Cup without him, and his team missed the playoffs. He said, 'Gretz, you'll miss the players, the friendships and the fans, but you won't even look back. It's just nice to go somewhere and be appreciated.'"

Gretzky and his wife moved into Canadian actor Alan Thicke's L.A. house while awaiting word on the progress of negotiations. Pocklington and Oiler coach-general manager Glen Sather had gone fishing at the end of July in the Northwest Territories with Sinden. When they got back, Carson, who had not been mentioned in McNall's and Pocklington's initial discussions, was the make-or-break player in the deal. "Sather obviously got involved during that fishing trip," says Gretzky. "That's why he's the best G.M. in the business."

When the word came, it came suddenly. In a late-night call that lasted into the wee hours of Tuesday, Aug. 9, the two owners finally came to terms. Some specifics of the trade had already leaked, so McNall and Pocklington decided on a press conference that afternoon. McNall woke Gretzky with a phone call and told him they were flying to Edmonton in his private plane that morning. "I can't," was Gretzky's initial reaction. "I'm not ready for this."

But he was. A few minutes before they were due at the press conference in Edmonton's Molson House, Pocklington, perhaps sensing for the first time the enormity of the transaction, gave Gretzky the chance to call off the trade. Gretzky declined. Then he had a brief tearful meeting with Sather. "It was out of Slats's hands," Gretzky says. "He didn't want to make the deal. He told me that."

When Pocklington's newly-hired personal publicist, Jeff Goodman, suggested that Pocklington and Gretzky ride over to the press conference together, buddy-buddy fashion. Gretzky refused. He also took offense that Goodman had written a statement for him to read. Speaking without a prepared text, Gretzky told the hushed assemblage of 200 reporters that he had requested the move to L.A. "for the benefit of Wayne Gretzky, my new wife and our expected child in the New Year. I feel I'm still young enough and capable enough to help a new franchise win the Stanley Cup." As he began to express his thanks to the people of Edmonton, he struggled and choked back the tears. "It's disappointing having to leave Edmonton...like I said, there comes a time when...." Then he stopped, unable to go on.

McNall and Gretzky flew back to L.A. that evening for a more upbeat news conference at the Sheraton Plaza La Reina, where Gretzky modeled the Kings' new silver, white and black uniform adorned by the number 99. The Kings, who have never advanced past the second round of the playoffs, were suddenly the talk of the town. All 8,500 loge seats in the Forum sold out for the season within three days of the Gretzky announcement. Prime Ticket, the cable outfit that televises Kings games, announced it would carry 60 this season, 33 more than in 1987–88.

Back in Edmonton, Pocklington dug himself an even deeper hole by telling *The Edmonton Journal* on Wednesday that Gretzky "has an ego the size of Manhattan.... He's a great actor. I thought he pulled it off beautifully when he showed how upset he was."

Pocklington later called Gretzky to apologize, claiming the remarks were taken out of context. "I understood where he was coming from when he talked about the size of my ego," Gretzky says. "He didn't mean that as an insult. But the part about the theatrics made me sick. I wouldn't accept an apology on that."

So who got the best of the trade? The big winner is the league, which suddenly finds its most glamorous player in its most glamour-starved market. If anyone can sell NHL hockey to the West Coast, it is Gretzky. Unfortunately, his presence in L.A. will do little to promote the sport nationally; the NHL, displaying an uncanny knack for shooting itself in the foot, recently rejected ESPN's bid to carry its games on cable in favor of SportsChannel, a regional cable company that will not penetrate markets where the league is traditionally weak.

As for the Oilers, their future is now secure. Those stockpiled draft choices ensure that they will be competitive into the next century. But being competitive is not the same as winning a Stanley Cup.

Conventional wisdom holds that the team that gets the best player gets the best of the trade. In this case that would be the Kings. A player like Gretzky brings the best out of everyone around him, so that the Kings may end up with 18 new players instead of three. Los Angeles still desperately needs help with goaltending and defense – Gretzky won't help them there – but McNall may not be through dealing. "We're still one or two players away," says Gretzky, a bit optimistically, "But if they hadn't made this deal I can guarantee you one thing: The Kings would have finished third or fourth and then been eliminated in the first round of the playoffs."

Very few in L.A. would have noticed. Now the entire country is watching, and a lot of folks are wishing them luck.

The effects of "The Trade" are still felt to this day. With Gretzky's tireless promotion in the south, the NHL was able to expand to new markets, with three teams now in California alone.

A KING IN EDMONTON

BY AUSTIN MURPHY | OCTOBER 31, 1988

*Wayne Gretzky returned to his old city and, though
initially uncertain about his old fan's reaction, was
greeted with heartfelt cheers*
(Photograph by Ken Levine/Getty Images)

WAYNE GRETZKY WAS BACK IN EDMONTON LAST WEEK, an outsider visiting the city he put on the map. The question hovering over the Great One's return was not whether his new team, the Los Angeles Kings, would beat his old one. The Kings didn't, bowing 8–6 to the Stanley Cup champion Oilers, although a rudderless (read: Gretzkyless) Edmonton power play kept the game closer than it should have been.

No, the reason all of hockeydom was riveted to this otherwise unremarkable – indeed, this downright sloppy – early-season shootout was to see whether Gretzky would be booed or cheered by the people of Edmonton. And how long would the booing or cheering last?

Ten weeks had passed since number 99 tearfully announced the fateful news that he and his pregnant bride, Janet Jones, whom he married on July 16, would be moving to a Southern California zip code. The resulting maelstrom of ill will swirled mainly around Jones, who was assumed to relish living in L.A. over Edmonton. Jones, an actress, was portrayed as the worst kind of dynasty wrecker until it was revealed that the deal had been initiated by none other than the Oilers' owner, Peter Pocklington, who felt he could get top dollar for Gretzky by unloading him before the Great One became a free agent in 1992.

Pocklington's image was further tarnished when it came to light that he had shopped Gretzky around before striking the deal with Los Angeles. Furious, Edmonton fans took to burning Pocklington in effigy.

For his part, Gretzky settled with his wife in the L.A. community of Encino and raved about his new surroundings. The Kings, he said, are "a great bunch of guys"; his "sensitive" new owner, Bruce McNall, "cares more about you as a person than he does about winning"; his adopted city is beautiful; traffic is "not that bad – if you drive at the right time. It's great going home from the game with the top down."

Gretzky looked forward to Wednesday night's game in Edmonton with something less than relish. It was not the pressure or scrutiny that had him spooked – he described the matchup as "just another one of those 'everybody's-watching games" – but rather the idea of playing against his best friends.

"I'd really rather not have to go in there," said Gretzky, with a sigh. "We were the closest team, I think, that's ever been assembled in pro sports. It's going to be extremely tough."

Among those Gretzky would be facing was his former housemate and roommate on the road, Kevin Lowe. After the trade, Lowe had stopped talking to the press and gave up his weekly column for *The Edmonton Sun* . But Gretzky expected no quarter from Lowe. "I see myself going one-on-one with Kevin and getting knocked down in front of the net," Gretzky said. "I'm not looking forward to that."

Nor did he look forward to tangling with Mark Messier, his successor as the Oiler captain and, like Lowe, a member of the Gretzky-Jones wedding party. Shortly after the bombshell trade was announced, Messier had called a press conference. It was widely thought he intended to express his outrage at Pocklington, but at the 11th hour Messier canceled the session, presumably to keep peace with Pocklington, who, after all, was still his boss.

What gave the game against the Oilers added interest was that the Kings, thanks to Gretzky, had gone from being a poor-to-fair team to a fair-to-good one. They're certainly on their way to becoming a richer team. Indeed, the Kings stand a good chance of making money this year, after having lost between $3.7 million and $5 million in each of the past three seasons. It is estimated that Gretzky this season will generate an additional $15 million for McNall's and the league's coffers through increased ticket sales, greater licensing revenues and a sweetened cable television deal. The hottest piece of merchandise around is the new black, silver and white Kings jersey with Gretzky's famous 99 on the back. Everyone in L.A. seems to own one. In Edmonton, too.

Gretzky's arrival naturally charged up the Kings, who have always been the NHL's long-lost brothers, stuck out there in sunny California with nobody for company. In 1972, then Kings owner Jack Kent Cooke observed that there were supposed to be some 800,000 transplanted Canadians living in Southern California and that they all had moved there to get away from hockey. But Gretzky is King, and L.A. loves superstars, domestic or imported. "It is not just one new guy," says Kings defenseman Steve

Duchesne, a holdover from 1987–88. "It is 23 new guys."

In fact, the Kings got off to a 4–0 start, the best in the franchise's dismal 21-year history. Gretzky's coming out against Detroit in the Forum on Oct. 6 was like a Hollywood premiere, complete with klieg lights and megawatt celebrities, and the Great One delighted the assembled glitterati by scoring on his *first shot* in an 8–2 Kings victory. Then came home victories over Calgary, the New York Islanders and Boston, followed by a 4–1 loss to Philadelphia. Though they were competing against the Dodgers, the Kings averaged 13,778 for those five games, up 2,111 over last season's average, which was the second worst in the league. Better still, the Forum was abuzz with the sound of diehards explaining to newcomers the difference between icing and offsides.

Then the schedule played a dirty trick on the Kings: It sent them on the road. Their first trip took them to Calgary, where on Oct. 17 the Flames' notoriously accomplished Gretzky-baiting fans accorded him a disorienting 20-second ovation. They probably were relieved that Gretzky was playing for L.A., not for their Alberta nemesis to the north. It was kinder treatment than the Kings received on the ice, where they were routed by the Flames 11–4.

L.A. trailed just 4–3 going into the last period; three of the Flames' seven third-period goals came within 60 seconds. Kings coach Robbie Ftorek kept goalie Rollie Melanson in the game all the way, later arguing, with some justification, that Melanson had not played poorly, 11 goals or no. Also distinguishing themselves for L.A. were defensemen Ken Baumgartner, who took six penalties, and Larry Playfair, who flung a cooler of chilled pucks from the penalty box onto the ice, costing his team a two-minute bench minor that led to Calgary's 11th goal. McNall, for one, discerned something positive in Playfair's rebellion. "It was a good sign," the owner said. "This team has accepted losing in the past, and now it sees losing as unacceptable." (Two days later, Playfair was dealt to Buffalo for left wing Bob Logan and a ninth-round draft choice in 1989.)

After the game in Calgary, the Kings, glumly silent, piled into a chartered bus and motored the 185 miles to Edmonton, where they checked into the Westin and crashed. It was in the same hotel – in the Crown Suite that has also housed Queen Elizabeth II, for whom it was named, and her son and daughter-in-law the Prince and Princess of Wales – that Gretzky and Jones had spent their wedding night. But now, here was Gretzky, three months later at a press conference, hoping aloud that the boos he expected to hear when he stepped on the Northlands Coliseum ice Wednesday night wouldn't be "too terrible, but you never know."

The Oilers did not exactly savor the notion of having to clamp down hard on the guy who had scored or set up 1,669, or 48%, of their goals since 1979 and had led them to four Stanley Cups. "I've been wondering what I'm going to do the first time he comes up my wing." said hulking defenseman Steve Smith. "Do I take him hard into the boards? Do I just hold him?" And Oilers general manager and coach Glen Sather said, "I've got enough aggravation as it is. I sure wouldn't mind having this one over with."

The Oilers got off to their usual sluggish start this season. Goalie Grant Fuhr had reported overweight and then injured his knee. Glenn Anderson had no goals in the first six games. Jimmy Carson, the wunderkind center who came from Los Angeles in the Gretzky deal, was taking a long time to adjust to Edmonton's style of play; on a team of speed merchants, he seemed a half step slow. On Oct. 12, Vancouver won at Edmonton for the first time in 3½ years. The Oilers showed up for Gretzky's return with a 2–2–2 record and were coming off tie games against Winnipeg and Minnesota, two of the more underwhelming teams in the NHL.

"We're still a good team," said Edmonton co-coach John Muckler. "We used to be a great team."

For all of Gretzky's trepidations, it quickly became apparent that all the good citizens of Edmonton wanted was the chance to bid their favorite son a proper goodbye, something the midsummer night's deal had deprived them of. The Canadian Broadcasting Company switched a regular-season broadcast of *Hockey Night in Canada*, usually seen on Saturday, to midweek for the first time in that program's 37-year history. More than 200 media credentials were requested, about five times the usual number for a nonplayoff game. A local radio station invited listeners to call in and share their "favorite Gretzky moments from over the last 10 years."

"I remember the time he gave the Stanley Cup to Marty McSorley, and Marty skated over and gave it to his dad...."

"I remember the time he tried to scrap with Neal Broten, and it looked like they were dancing...."

And so forth. Listeners who contributed the best Gretzky memories were awarded copies of the Pink Floyd album *Momentary Lapse of Reason*. The night of the big game, the cover charge at Goose Loonies, a nightclub over on Edmonton's south side, was 99 cents.

Did Gretzky really think he might be booed? The instant he stepped on the ice for the pregame skate, he was showered with full-throated expressions of adoration. Later, the cheers came to a deafening crescendo when the Kings took the ice just before the national anthems. For almost four minutes, 17,503 people stood as one and paid lusty tribute. Would they cheer? Indeed. Would they ever stop?

The love-in might have lasted much longer had not Oiler officials, trying to act as though nothing extraordinary were afoot, trundled out Edmontonian Tim Feehan to sing the national anthems right on schedule. But the real wet blanket was Ftorek, who didn't put Gretzky among the first five Kings to take the ice. No matter. Everyone present knew what was happening. Pocklington looked down from his luxury box with McNall at his side. When asked if he would sit with Pocklington, McNall had said, "As long as the glass is bulletproof."

DOWN THE DRAIN WITHOUT WAYNE prophesied one gloomy sign. Wrong. With Melanson still shell-shocked from his misadventure in Calgary. Ftorek went with Glenn Healy in the net, and Healy promptly let six of the Oilers' first 15 shots get behind him. Not that he was entirely to blame. As had been the case in Calgary, the Kings defensemen were abominable.

And Gretzky was a little too keyed up. He did have two assists, but he misfired or was robbed by Fuhr on his four strong scoring chances. The one-on-one confrontation that both Gretzky and Lowe dreaded didn't come off, as Lowe, still woozy from a concussion suffered in a game against Calgary the previous week, sat out. But Messier, with whom Gretzky would share a quiet meal after the game, wasted no time depositing 99 on the seat of his shiny new black shorts. He later devoured the Kings' helpless defensemen, scoring on two of his patented rocket-wrist shots, the first while the Oilers were short-handed, to put them up 4–1.

Damned if L.A. would roll over, though. Every time it looked as though the rout was on, some non-Gretzky King would pop a goal and keep the visitors in it. Still, no matter how close the Kings came this night, one suspected that Messier would never let his team lose.

"Down the right side, snap the puck in – I've seen him do it a hundred times." said Gretzky of his successor's first goal. "Mess is a great, great hockey player," continued the Great One, a twinkle in his eye. "I just wish he was for sale."

After a slow start, the Gretzky-led Kings would turn things around en route to their first winning season in four years.

WHERE HE REIGNS, GOALS POUR

BY AUSTIN MURPHY | DECEMBER 19, 1988

With Wayne Gretzky as their new captain, the Kings turned around their fortunes and found themselves playing like royalty

(Photograph by Mike Powell/Getty Images)

SO HOW ARE THINGS WITH THE NEW KING OF L.A., WAYNE Gretzky? In a word, terrific. The Kings are winning games at a rate unprecedented in the franchisees 22-year history, and owner Bruce McNall, who in August shelled out $15 million for Gretzky, is getting a handsome return on his investment far sooner than expected.

If the Kings seem surprised by their 19–10–1 record, it is probably because two decades of lopsided losses have accustomed them to life in or near the Smythe Division cellar. And let's face it, even with the Great One and the six other players the Kings acquired in the off-season, nobody figured L.A. would be contending for first place in the division in mid-December. "It's not going to happen overnight." Gretzky had said in the preseason – and he was right. It took close to a week.

The Kings jumped out to a 4–0 start before tailing off in mid-October with losses to the division's elite teams, Calgary and Edmonton, by a combined score of 19–10. Since then, though, L.A. has been one of hockey's hottest outfits, winning 12 of its last 17 games, scoring goals by the bushel and drawing larger crowds than ever before.

Gretzky – and most everybody else – had underestimated

the magnitude of the effect he would have. Says left wing Luc Robitaille, "You see him working so hard every *second*. This is the best player in the world, so how can you not *try* to work that hard?"

Robitaille is also grateful that opponents' top checking units are usually preoccupied with trying to stop Gretzky. That frees Luc and his linemates, center Bernie Nicholls and wing Dave Taylor, to wreak some havoc. L.A. had scored 157 goals before its 4–3 win over the plummeting New York Islanders last Saturday, by far the most in the league (the Oilers, still smarting from the absence of a certain someone, were a distant second in goals, with 146, and were *third* in the division standings, behind Calgary and L.A.). Ripples of the Gretzky Effect were touching everyone on the team. Glenn Healy's goals-against average, a pedestrian 3.97, put him in the middle of the pack among NHL goalies, but because the guys in front of him were averaging more than five goals a game, he led the league in wins, with 14.

Steve Duchesne, the Kings' slick offensive defenseman, had a plus-38 rating, the best plus-minus mark in the league – and in the history of the Kings. Nicholls is the most dramatic example of a King whose play has been elevated by Gretzky. "Wayne has been Wayne and Bernie has been, well, incredible," says team captain Taylor Nicholls, 27, was the NHL's third-leading point scorer, with 33 goals and 37 assists at week's end, behind Gretzky and Pittsburgh's Mario Lemieux.

"Playing with Wayne is one of the most exciting things that has ever happened to me," says Nicholls. In 1980, as a 19-year-old junior hockey star, Nicholls scored 152 points for the Kingston Canadians, and his future looked golden. But that year the Kings selected him in the entry draft.

From 1982 to 1988 Nicholls scored 36 goals a year and earned a reputation for durability. He broke his jaw in January 1984 and played the rest of the season with his mouth wired shut. Last season, when Nicholls missed 10 games because of a broken finger, he ended a three-and-a-half-year playing streak of 267 consecutive games.

"I paid my dues." he says. "We were a lousy team for a long time. We would be out of the playoff picture by January or February."

Nicholls's eight points in a 9–3 win over Toronto on Dec. 1 broke a club record. But it's important to note that his first goal in the Leaf game, a splendid, shorthanded effort, could have been set up by only one man. Ragging the puck, keeping it away from two Toronto players in his own end, Gretzky appeared to be gazing into the Forum's cheap seats when he suddenly wristed a 70-foot pass to Nicholls, who gathered it at center ice and converted the breakaway.

At Gretzky's request, his roommate on the road this season is the enigmatic Bob Carpenter. L.A. is Carpenter's third stop in his eight years in the NHL; both of his previous clubs, the Washington Capitals and the New York Rangers, called him a disappointment before unloading him. In the 1984–85 season he scored 53 goals for the Caps, but in the next three seasons he had 27, nine and 19. If he is ever to regain his old form, it will be as Gretzky's left wing.

"Maybe he did get lucky a few times the year he got 53," says Gretzky. "But Bobby is a legitimate 40-goal scorer."

Carpenter, 25, is clearly buoyed by Gretzky's faith in him. "Wayne has helped me in a lot of ways," says Carpenter. "Just by his being here, we have 20 new players; it's like we're a different team in the same city."

Still, things in L.A. are not entirely rosy. Gretzky and coach Robbie Ftorek have struck sparks off one another. An incident during L.A.'s 8–3 romp over Detroit in Joe Louis Arena on Nov. 23 fueled a firestorm of speculation. Frustrated after being fleeced of the puck by the Red Wings' Steve Yzerman, who then scored, Gretzky smashed his stick against the crossbar. Ftorek benched him for eight minutes, even though Gretzky already had five assists and a goal – the 600th of his NHL career – in the game. To add to Gretzky's embarrassment, a contingent of his family and friends had made the 150-mile drive from Brantford, Ont., for the game.

"I'm sorry about that, Wayne," Ftorek reportedly told Gretzky after benching him, "but I'm trying to teach these guys some composure."

"If you want to teach...teach in New Haven," Gretzky reportedly replied. "We're trying to win a Stanley Cup."

Ftorek refused to elaborate on what later happened. "What's said in the dressing room stays in the dressing room," he says. "Its family stuff." Gretzky would only say that the incident has been "totally exaggerated."

Another possible pitfall for the Kings is the level of competition in the Smythe. The Kings are a sterling 16–3 outside the division and 3–7–1 within (1–4 against Calgary and Edmonton). But Gretzky is thoroughly upbeat. "What we lack right now is patience," he says. "We've got to have the confidence to know that if we're down 2–1 or

3–2 in a game, we don't have to take chances. We're going to score goals."

Nicholls, for one, is ready to do just that. The day after his eight-point dissection of the Leafs, he admitted he had been too excited to sleep. "You have to understand," he said, with the giddiness of a child on Christmas morning, "I haven't had many highlights in my career."

The Kings continued on a tear for the remainder of the 1988–89 regular season, ending up in second place in the Smythe Division, but leading the league in goals scored with 376. The Great One accounted for 54 of them.

DYNASTY UNDONE

BY AUSTIN MURPHY | APRIL 24, 1989

In a week marked by tragedy and triumph, Wayne Gretzky's heroics in the Stanley Cup playoffs stood out as Los Angeles beat Edmonton
(Photograph by Robert Riger/Getty Images)

LET POSTERITY NOTE THAT THE EDMONTON OILER DYNASTY expired last Saturday at 10:29 p.m., Pacific daylight time. The mortal blow, though, had been struck eight months earlier, on Aug. 9, 1988. That was the day Wayne Gretzky became a Los Angeles King and the day a great team, the Oilers – winners of four Stanley Cups in five seasons – became merely a good one.

Winning a playoff series without Gretzky in itself presented a difficult task for the Oilers; winning one *against* him – even after sitting on a fat three-games-to-one lead in their Smythe Division semifinal series – proved not to be in the cards. "I told our guys once we went up three-one, 'Don't start thinking that it's over,'" said a grim Glen Sather, Edmonton's general manager and coach, after the Oilers were eliminated 6–3 in Saturday's Game 7. "You got a player like Wayne on a club, that club is not going to fold."

Shockingly, it was the Oilers who folded, after skating to that supposedly daunting lead, a choke of such colossal proportions that it has been duplicated only five times in NHL history.

In victory, Gretzky, who assisted on the game-winner

and scored two other goals in the clincher – one of them just 52 seconds into the game – was the picture of graciousness and conciliation. "No one takes losing worse than Mark Messier and Kevin Lowe," he said of his close friends and former Edmonton teammates. "Long after hockey's done and over with, Kevin and Mark and I will still be buddies."

Gretzky's guard slipped just once, at a mention of Oiler owner Peter Pocklington, with whom he has feuded since Pocklington dealt him to the Kings. "He said after Game 3 that the people of Edmonton had told him the trade was a good trade," said Gretzky. "We'll see what they say tomorrow."

How did the Kings – written off by nearly everyone last week – come back? For one, goalie Kelly Hrudey kicked the flu that had kept him out of Game 1 and limited his effectiveness until Game 5. His counterpart on the Oilers, Grant Fuhr, who had sparkled in the early going, stealing Games 1 and 3 for Edmonton, could not sustain his early brilliance. In Games 5 through 7, it was Hrudey's turn to confound and amaze his opponents.

Hrudey's most memorable moment in the seventh game came in the final minute of the second period. Edmonton's Craig Simpson – who had brashly predicted as the Oilers skated out for pregame warmups, "I got the game-winner tonight" – broke in alone on Hrudey, who fell on his back kicking out Simpson's first shot. In one fluid motion, Simpson pounced on his own rebound and wristed it high. From a supine position, Hrudey threw up his right arm and miraculously stopped the sure goal with his forearm, after which he smothered the puck.

That was only one of the frustrating moments for the Oilers – the fastest-skating team in the league – who were unable to get out of second gear all night. Some of the credit for this goes to Kings coach Robbie Ftorek, who instructed his forwards to fall back quickly on defense and clog the neutral zone – that area between the blue lines where the Oilers gear up their attack. Credit also Kings center Steve Kasper, who as a Boston Bruin had gained renown for his ability to frustrate Gretzky. On Saturday it was Kasper's assignment to check Messier, and while Edmonton's captain did assist on all three goals, Kasper was in his sweater so often that Messier could never take off on one of his rink-length rushes.

Great goaltending and enterprising D were not all that the new Kings seemed to borrow from the old Oilers. Edmonton's playoff teams of recent vintage always seemed to get important goals from obscure and unexpected sources. Last week it was a cast of unlikely Kings wearing the mantle of hero.

There was Mike Allison, a plumber's plumber, carrying Oiler defenseman Randy Gregg 15 yards along the end-boards before lunging toward the net and sweeping the puck between Fuhr's skates to tie Game 6, 1–1. Last summer it had been Allison, upon hearing that Gretzky would be a teammate, who said, "They finally got someone who can skate with me." He was joking. Of his game-tying goal, Allison said, "It wasn't anything pretty." He was right. It was just clutch.

So was Jim Wiemer's wrist shot from a tough angle at 4:14 of the third period, which proved to be the game-winner. Wiemer had spent most of his season with the Cape Breton

(Nova Scotia) Oilers in Edmonton's minor league system. In March, Sather traded Wiemer to L.A. and then told the *Los Angeles Times* he had no qualms about the deal because Wiemer was old and slow. Nothing wrong with his wrist shot though, eh, Slats?

Finally there was the curious case of Chris Kontos, who was a first-round draft pick of the New York Rangers in 1982. A left wing who earned a rep for having an "attitude problem," he spent time in the minors in each of the six previous seasons and admits, "I made some mistakes. I'd rather not discuss them now." He ended up playing in Switzerland this season.

In six games with the Kings last year, Kontos had a dozen points, yet Kings general manager Rogie Vachon wouldn't promise him employment for the new season. This March, when the season ended for his Swiss team, Kontos offered his services, and Vachon decided to sign him. Easier said than done. The Kings faxed a copy of the contract to the only place they could find with a fax machine in Kontos's hometown of Midland, Ont. – Beaver Lumber. Kontos signed it, and the lumberyard faxed a copy to the league office minutes before the free-agent signing deadline.

It was worth the trouble. When Bernie Nicholls's slap shot ricocheted off Kontos's arm and into the net, giving the Kings a 2–1 lead on Saturday, it was Kontos's eighth goal of the playoffs, tops in the league. Not too shabby for a guy who spent most of the regular season playing in Europe.

Angelenos thrilled to the comeback. Before Game 5, Ftorek read a letter from that renowned rightwinger, Ronald Reagan, who exhorted the Kings to – what else – "Win one for the Gipper!" They did, by a score of 4–2.

When the Kings returned from Edmonton for Saturday's seventh game, their dressing room was adorned with bouquets of balloons sent by Magic Johnson. Once the game began, Kathleen Turner, Jack Nicholson, Sly Stallone and various other indigenous luminaries offered vocal support.

But when Stallone's name was flashed on the Forum's message board, it received only a fraction of the applause accorded an employee of L.A. radio station KLOS, a gentleman known only as Robert "the Lucky Butt."

Hours before Game 5, with the Forum still empty, the Lucky Butt was escorted to center ice, where he dropped his trousers and pressed his bare buns to the face-off circle.

The Kings won, so KLOS flew Robert to Edmonton, where he repeated his strange rite. "Kind of gives you goose bumps just thinking about it," said Kings captain Dave Taylor.

The Lucky Butt made a third appearance Saturday, but seemed to have exhausted its powers late in the second period. With the game tied 3–3 and the Kings on the power play, John Tonelli scored cleanly on a blistering slap shot from the point. Alas, the puck hit a pipe that runs down the back of the goal and bounced out. Though this was evident on TV replays, it happened too fast for the goal judge, and the Kings were robbed of a goal.

Perhaps to make amends, referee Andy Van Hellemond – who has been called Van Solomon for his creative adjudications – gave Edmonton's Craig Muni a holding penalty mere seconds after the nongoal. On the ensuing five-on-three, Gretzky easily fed Nicholls for the game-winner.

The Oilers, not surprisingly, did not go gentle into that

good off-season. Late in the final period, to stop play and get a breather, Lowe gambled and knocked his own net off its moorings. He was called for delay of game, and the Kings' Dale DeGray pumped in an insurance goal while Lowe looked helplessly on. For what seemed like a long time after that goal, Lowe sat on the bench, staring blankly ahead. Fuhr, meanwhile, flung his stick at the sideboards, furious that Van Hellemond had not called Taylor for interfering with him.

After he had showered, Messier's route to the bus took him past the Kings' dressing room. He did not poke his head in to say hello.

"I saw those guys every day, and yet we didn't speak," said Gretzky. "That's not what life is supposed to be about. You're supposed to be able to talk to your best friends. Those two, Kevin and Mark, are the ones I feel most sorry for. They are champions."

Correction: *were* champions. The Great One helped see to that.

The Kings' opponent in the Smythe Division final is that other Alberta team, the Calgary Flames, who advanced after winning a seventh-game overtime heartstopper 4–3 over the plucky Vancouver Canucks. One waggish Vancouver columnist had predicted that the Canucks would be ousted from the best-of-seven series in three games, but it took heroic goaltending by Calgary's Mike Vernon to keep the supposedly mighty Flames from being snuffed out.

Calgary went into the series with the NHL's best regular-season record, 54–17–9 – 43 points and 103 goals better than Vancouver. The Canucks hadn't made the playoffs the two previous seasons, and they had won only three playoff series in their history, all in 1981–82, when they lost to the New York Islanders in the Stanley Cup finals. But they kept coming at the Flames, winning at home on Thursday night 6–3 to force a seventh game.

And they would have won that one but for Vernon, who turned away 11 shots in OT before center Joel Otto scored the series-winner at 19:21. Three of those shots not only could have made losers of Calgary, they *should* have. In order, Vernon kicked out his left skate to just get a toe on a shot by Petri Skriko at 5:15, stopped a breakaway at 14:30 when he gloved Stan Smyl's slap shot to the lower right corner, and snared Tony Tanti's blast from 35 feet with a flick of his glove at 15:24.

Otto's winning goal wasn't a very comely one. "Who'd have believed that one would go in?" he said. He had stormed the net to create a little havoc when a centering pass from Jim Peplinski grazed off his skate past Canuck goalie Kirk McLean. Of fellow hero Vernon he said, "Vernie, he saves us. He was pulling pucks out of his ear all night."

The game was redemption of sorts for Vernon, who could have used a flak jacket to handle the strafing he received from Calgary fans and hockey writers when the Flames were chased from the divisional playoffs by provincial rival Edmonton last season and by Winnipeg the year before. "I worked hard all season, and it comes down to one period like that," said Vernon. "I thought to myself, I just can't let it end here. I just seemed to dig down and go to the well once more."

Vancouver players openly wept after the loss, but coach Bob McCammon said, "I told the guys they have nothing to be ashamed of. I can still see Smyl on that breakaway, Skriko with an open net. Oh boy, this was their lucky day. I believe the best team is going back to Vancouver."

And the lucky team was facing a King-sized challenge.

Calgary swept the Kings in the next round en route to a Stanley Cup championship. The next year, the Gretzky-less Oilers' dynasty collected one last Cup before trades and age finally broke it up.

A BACKHANDED COMPLIMENT

BY JAY GREENBERG | OCTOBER 23, 1989

In breaking Gordie Howe's scoring record, Wayne Gretzky honored Howe by using the shot he told Gretzky to perfect

(Photograph by DK Photo/Getty Images)

WHEN 11-YEAR-OLD WAYNE GRETZKY MET GORDIE HOWE at a sports awards banquet in 1972, Howe gave him a piece of advice: Work on your backhand. Fast forward to Sunday, Oct. 15, 1989. Gretzky takes the puck on that backhand and flips it into the net with 53 seconds left in the Los Angeles Kings' game with the Oilers at Edmonton's Northlands Coliseum. In that instant, the NHL career scoring record of 1,850 points that Howe built over 26 seasons was surpassed.

Gretzky had tied the record with an assist early in the game, but as time ticked away in the third period, it had appeared that the mark would not be broken this night in this place, with its strong ties to Gretzky. Then, suddenly, there was that Howe-recommended backhand, which Gretzky had practiced at home with a tennis ball only a zillion times or so.

Gretzky's momentous shot not only broke Howe's record but also tied the game 4–4. He then won the game for the Kings in overtime with still another goal, and he did all this against his old teammates, in the city where he led the Oilers to four Stanley Cups before being traded to Los Angeles last year. And he did it in 780 games to Howe's 1,767.

The record breaking almost had to wait for Game 781,

because what had been a wide-open game settled down in the second period, and so did Edmonton goalie Bill Ranford, who twice made strong pad saves against Gretzky during a 5-on-3 L.A. advantage. In addition, Gretzky suffered mild dizziness from a bump on the head in the second period, and coach Tom Webster held him out for a few shifts. When Ranford stopped a Gretzky-fed Bernie Nicholls shot on a power play with two minutes to go in the third period, there was a feeling that, well, nobody comes through on cue every time, not even the greatest player who ever lived.

But then Gretzky did deliver. Teammate Steve Duchesne saved a clearing attempt by Edmonton's Kevin Lowe and whacked the puck toward the crease, where it hit Kings winger Dave Taylor on the leg and came right to Gretzky on the left side of the goal. "I don't know what made me go there," said Gretzky. "I'm usually the outlet guy [in back of the net]."

What made him go there were the best instincts in the history of the game, and what made the Coliseum erupt in tumultuous cheers was a bond that Gretzky's trade to the Kings has not severed. The game was interrupted for a presentation of gifts from the NHL, the Oilers and the Kings. When it resumed, and Gretzky scored the overtime winner, Howe said, "There is no end to Wayne's brilliance." The magnificence of the moment may even have warmed the cool relations between Gretzky and Oilers' owner Peter Pocklington, who offered his congratulations out of public view after the game.

Gretzky's accomplishments have been so astonishing that they have acquired a mystical aura. It was suggested

during the countdown to the record that destiny was guid-
ing events so that the payoff points would come in
Edmonton. More certain than the hands of fate, however,
are the hands of Gretzky. He came into this season having
averaged 2.37 points a game for his career. At that rate,
needing 14 points to break the record, he would reach
1,851 in game 6. The fact that game 6 was to be played in
Edmonton met the league's schedule, and Gretzky's, and
destiny's.

The possibility – nay, probability – of getting his 1,851st
at his old home rink was not lost on Gretzky. He mentioned
the Kings' Oct. 15 visit to Northlands Coliseum as early as
June, at the NHL awards ceremony, where he received his
ninth Hart Trophy as the league's MVP. Of course, when
Gretzky was asked where he really wanted to set the record,
he always carefully considered the feelings of Bruce McNall,
the owner of the Kings, and the Forum faithful. "My first
choice is to do it in Los Angeles," Gretzky said. "If I can't,
I'd like to do it in Edmonton."

Anyone who remembered how Gretzky became the first
NHL player ever to score 50 goals in fewer than the first
50 games of a season, in 1981, certainly didn't discount his
chances of getting the record even before he arrived in
Edmonton. After 38 games in 1981 Gretzky needed only
five goals to reach 50, and on the morning of game 39 he
told his roommate, Kevin Lowe, that he thought he could
get all five that evening at home against the Philadelphia
Flyers. And darned if he didn't. His fifth, an empty-netter,
came in the final minute.

So Howe, who was invited by McNall to travel with the

Kings during the chase, didn't risk arriving too late. On Oct. 8, he was seated in McNall's box at the Forum for the Kings' third game of the season, in which Gretzky had three assists against the Detroit Red Wings. Two nights later Gretzky added a goal and two assists at home against the New York Islanders and was only five shy of the record when he got to Vancouver for last Friday's game.

Gretzky has scored five points in one game 58 times in his career, but he settled for a mere three against the Canucks, including an eyes-in-the-back-of-his-head pass around defenseman Robert Nordmark to Steve Kasper to set up the game-winner with one second left.

Howe claimed to have no inside word as to when the record breaker might come, but he did drop a hint in Vancouver that he might be in the know. He showed up for the Kings' game against the Canucks in a turquoise sport coat. "If I thought he was going to do it tonight, I would have worn a suit," Howe said. "The suit will be on in Edmonton."

That wasn't the first time during the week a future Howe wardrobe had become an object of speculation. Five nights earlier he had suggested to the media that he might put on a uniform again after New Year's, at age 61, to fulfill a desire to play NHL hockey in each of six decades.

Howe first retired from the NHL in 1971, after 25 years with the Red Wings; he came back two seasons later to play in the World Hockey Association for the Houston Aeros and the New England Whalers for six years with his sons Marty and Mark. He then rejoined the NHL for one last hurrah, at age 51, with the Hartford Whalers in 1979–80.

The Los Angeles papers noted the frivolous nature of Howe's comments about un-retiring, but a Detroit paper took them seriously. Suddenly, Howe became interested. "The general public evidently is excited," he said. "And it does make you feel good." On Oct. 11, Howe's wife, Colleen, had a statement read to the press in which she downplayed this "fantasy," but then she added to the confusion by going to the podium and saying, "If he's going to get in shape for one game, he might as well play a season."

Gretzky, who began his professional career in 1978 with the Indianapolis Racers of the WHA and thus got to play three games alongside Howe on an All-Star team in a 1979 series against Moscow Dynamo, said he thought a Howe comeback was a great idea. "If Gordie wants to play, I'm sure he can," said Gretzky.

Well, if Gretzky has taken up the misguided notion that a 61-year-old man can still be competitive with elite athletes in their 20s, he should be indulged. His clouded thinking is the result of almost 25 years of acute hero worship.

It was Howe, after all, who rescued the 11-year-old Gretzky when the young hockey prodigy was suffering from stage fright at that banquet in Brantford, Ont. Howe had jumped up, put his arm around Gretzky and announced, "When someone has done what this kid has done in the rink, he doesn't have to say anything." What the kid had done that year was score 378 goals in 82 games for the sub-peewee level Brantford Steelers.

It was also Howe who a few years later told the adolescent Gretzky that he had two eyes and one mouth and that the best advice he could give him was to keep the two open and the one closed. And it was Howe who, in that 1979 series against the Soviets, told Gretzky to get the opening face-off back to Mark Howe and then go to the net. Mark would throw it into the corner, where Gordie would retrieve it and get it to Gretzky in front of the goal. In 10 seconds the puck was there for an easy tap-in.

And there was another lesson Gretzky would always remember. In the first WHA game he ever played against Howe, he stole the puck from his idol. Gretzky was wheeling back up ice, feeling very much like a legend-to-be, when he suddenly felt a sharp whack on his thumb. When he looked up, the old coot – always known for the crafty use of his stick – was winking at him.

Gretzky never saw a record he didn't want to break, but he wishes somebody else had owned this one. He insists that Howe will always be the greatest. Uneasy at the thought of diminishing a legend, Gretzky told Howe months ago it would mean a lot to him if he could be there when – gee, Gordie, sorry – the inevitable occurred.

Howe was equally gracious. "I kissed that record good-bye a long time ago, when Wayne started getting 200 points a year," said Howe. "He's good and I know, because I played with him. If you want to tell me he's the greatest player of all time, I have no argument at all."

Like its holder, Howe's record had been built to last. He dominated the corners – and didn't cut many either on the way to scoring his 1,850 points. All but the last five of his 26 NHL seasons were played in a fiercely competitive six-team league, where defenders gave up few easy goals.

Mr. Hockey had the arms of a lumberjack, and the callous disregard of one, too, for any limbs that might get in the way of his work. And yet Howe established the record – he became the NHL's career scoring leader in 1960 when he passed Montreal Canadien Maurice Richard's total of 965 points – with the patience and concentration of an architect. "He was in control of the whole game," says Gretzky, who watched Howe on TV in his prime. "He seemed to do everything so gracefully."

Howe averaged 30 goals and 40 assists a year for those 26 seasons. He never scored 50 goals, but only in his first three seasons and his final one did he score fewer than 20. He played a full decade before slap shots became common and almost another 10 years after that before defensemen started to join the attack. Only in the last four NHL seasons before his first retirement were there expansion teams like the California Golden Seals to pile up goals on, making 100-point seasons possible. Howe didn't have one of those until 1968–69, the second season after the league doubled in size. He was 41 years old then, good as always, but more remarkable than ever.

"I don't care how far past his record I go, he'll always be the greatest player who ever lived," says Gretzky. "And the classiest, too. See, one of the great things about him is that he doesn't get into comparing eras. You'll never get him to say that the competition now is watered down.

"It bothers me, sure, when I hear that. Obviously, the game is not as defensively oriented as it was in his day. The defensemen almost never came up past the blue line. Offensive players were never used to kill penalties. But you won't get Gordie to say now that the game used to be better. Because it wasn't. I can see how it has improved just from when I came into the league. I'd see a 6'3" defenseman then and I figured I could have a field day because he couldn't move. Now they're that size, but mobile and smart too. The skill level is higher now than it was 20 years ago, and 20 years from now it'll be higher than it is now."

When it reaches that point, Gretzky will continue to be a marvel. Fortune has delivered to the same era two play-ers – Gretzky and the Pittsburgh Penguins' Mario Lemieux – who are far and away the most prolific scorers in the game's history. That says something about the era, of course. But the points Lemieux and Gretzky are running up also may show that presumed performance limits in hockey are not physiological but psychological. Lemieux, a hugely productive but still underachieving talent in his first three NHL seasons, was finally challenged by Gretzky to be as good as he could be when they played on the same line in the 1987 Canada Cup. Lemieux has outscored Gretzky in the two years thereafter.

And it should not be forgotten that Gretzky is only 28. If he averages 160 points over the last seven years of his cur-rent contract, he will have 2,957. To beat that, Lemieux, now 24, would need 187 per season for 12 years. "I think if Mario stays healthy, he has a chance," Gretzky said last week.

If he does, he will not only have to be as skilled as Gretzky, but he'll also have to care for the game as much too. Last week the energy, the sheer joy of playing that passed from Howe to Gretzky when he was just a kid, were returned as Gretzky unselfishly turned this record for the ages into a celebration of Howe. "Thank God Wayne is the person he is," said Colleen, "because he is bigger than the league. He is what hockey is today."

He remains, too, as grateful for his gifts as the game is to have him. Because of that, the flame from the torch that was passed Sunday night between two legends was especially warming.

Gretzky's scoring pace slowed over his final years – he wouldn't make 2,957 in seven years as predicted. He did, however, end his career with 2,857 points, besting Gordie Howe's combined NHL/WHA points total along the way.

ONLY MORTAL AFTER ALL?

BY JAY GREENBERG | FEBRUARY 26, 1990

After 10 seasons, Wayne Gretzky started to feel the wear and tear of life in the NHL. That spelled trouble for the Kings

(Photograph by Otto Greule Jr./Getty Images)

RUMORS THAT WAYNE GRETZKY IS HUMAN HAVE surfaced sporadically throughout his career, but they have always been easily refuted. One merely had to look at the NHL record book.

Gretzky holds 51 individual marks, which reflect his attainments on the ice. And until Jan. 20, the Saturday of the NHL All-Star weekend in Pittsburgh, he didn't have a single black mark off the ice. But that day, Gretzky slept in and missed a sold-out practice session, and his squeaky-clean image was tarnished. To make matters worse, he performed the next day as though his bones ached. While the Pittsburgh Penguins' Mario Lemieux scored four goals for his team, Gretzky produced none for his.

And now there are whispers that the Great One is in decline. By week's end the Los Angeles Kings were 4–8–1 since the All-Star Game, and Gretzky had scored a pedestrian total of 18 points. It is obvious that he is fatigued; his legs, which carried him to an average of 2.37 points per game coming into this season, lack spring, and his stick no longer owns the puck.

"Anybody who plays 25 minutes a game, as I do, always feels it at around the 55- to 60-game mark," he said. "But

I've probably been more tired than I've been in other years."

The Kings have tried to help Gretzky, who's 29, catch his breath by not double-shifting him on a fourth line. "If I was the coach, I'd use me on the fifth line," Gretzky said disgustedly after being held pointless in a 5–3 loss in Toronto on Feb. 12. "God, I'm tired of talking about losing."

To be fair, Gretzky doesn't get as much help in L.A. as he did with the Edmonton Oilers, who traded him to the Kings in August 1988. With a supporting cast in Edmonton that included Jari Kurri, Paul Coffey, Mark Messier and Glenn Anderson, Gretzky became a legend as an Oiler. But he is not quite the player he was when he scored more than 200 points in four out of five seasons between 1981–82 and 1985–86. Of course, Gretzky silenced his new critics last week – at least for the moment – when he had two goals and one assist in a 6–5 loss to the Detroit Red Wings and two goals and three assists in a 7–1 victory over the Quebec Nordiques.

A decline for Gretzky, mind you, would amount to a renaissance for most anybody else. Gretzky can talk about the 168 points he scored last season, which was the eighth highest total in the history of the NHL. And this season, he noted last week, "I'm only five points behind a guy [Lemieux] who is 24 years old and had a 46-game scoring streak. I must be doing something right."

But Lemieux, not Gretzky, won the Art Ross Trophy (for scoring) the past two seasons. And this season Lemieux not only led Gretzky in points by a healthy margin but also was within five games of one of Gretzky's most cherished records – his 51-game scoring streak – when he was stopped Feb. 14 by the New York Rangers and a herniated disk in his back. The only way Gretzky will reclaim the scoring title this season is if Lemieux is disabled for any length of time. And Gretzky's chances of winning a 10th Hart Trophy (most valuable player) in 11 years are about as good as those of his wife replacing ailing goalie Kelly Hrudey in the L.A. nets.

Sensitive to the rivalry between Lemieux and Gretzky, Kings owner Bruce McNall announced on Feb. 1 that last summer he extended the Great One's contract from seven years to nine years and raised its value from $20 million to $31.3 million. The new contract, an upgrade on the original eight-year deal Gretzky signed after being obtained from Edmonton, was agreed upon, but not finalized, before the NHL Players Association voted in October to publicly disclose all salaries. McNall pushed his attorneys to do the paperwork so that Gretzky's upgraded salary – $2.72 million a year, which includes $1 million in deferred income – would be the one disclosed. The package puts Gretzky ahead of Lemieux, who had become hockey's best-paid player when he signed a $2 million-a-year deal last August.

Whatever the standard of Gretzky's play at the moment, it would be wrong to suggest that he will not live happily ever after in Los Angeles. His wife, actress Janet Jones, sometimes itches to resume her acting career but has turned down television parts to spend more time with their 14-month-old daughter, Paulina. The Gretzkys are planning to have more children, and there are lots of rooms for kids in their big house in Encino. Gretzky also enjoys more privacy in L.A. than he did in Edmonton. There are a lot of places in L.A. where a hockey player, even *the* hockey player, can go unnoticed. "I'm only in the sports sections here," he says. "People won't know who our kids are. That wouldn't have been possible in Canada."

While Gretzky's endorsement revenue is up considerably since his move to a major U.S. market, his time spent being a celebrity may actually be down. Fatherhood is first on Gretzky's list of priorities, friends a close second. Shortly before the All-Star weekend, Denise Gendron of Edmonton, a dear friend of the Gretzkys' who spoke at their wedding, found that her leukemia was no longer in remission. "Janet has spent a lot of time there the last few weeks," says Gretzky, who has made a public appeal for a bone-marrow donor for Gendron. "Denise is a great girl. This has been hard on us."

So was the All-Star weekend, when Gretzky's best friend on the Kings, center Bernie Nicholls, was traded to the Rangers for right wings Tomas Sandstrom and Tony Granato. After hearing – and believing – the trade rumors upon his Friday arrival in Pittsburgh, Gretzky faced two options early the next morning: to get out of bed on the wrong side or not to get out at all.

"Saturday was a tough morning for me and my wife," he says. "And I thought it was an optional practice. I'll take full responsibility, but seven other players [still traveling to Pittsburgh after playing on Friday night] weren't there either. I get booed in Pittsburgh all the time. What would you rather do, stay in bed with your wife and daughter or get booed for another hour? Give me a break. The All-Star Game is supposed to be fun. I can't be excited about playing in it, when my best friend is being traded. Before I left for the game, I told Janet, 'I'm going to be awful today.'"

The Kings have been awful too, despite the deep pockets of McNall. Gretzky's work load remains much the same as it was in 1988–89, but the Kings have fallen back to fourth place in the Smythe Division. This hurts Gretzky, who, after being touted as the salvation of the franchise, understandably feels responsible.

McNall, who made his fortune dealing in old Greek and Roman coins, has too many ancient players on his roster to grind through the four playoff rounds required to win the Stanley Cup. There are seven Kings 30 or older, and not enough younger ones who take pride in their defensive work. Nicholls, who was the fourth-leading scorer in the NHL last season but was nonchalant when it came to practice and checking, fell victim to the Kings' need for better defense. Both Granato, who has played only one game since the trade because of a pulled groin muscle, and Sandstrom add speed and grit to the Kings. Sandstrom, moreover, could be the right wing the Kings have needed to complement Gretzky.

Nicholls, who centered a dangerous second line behind Gretzky, undoubtedly lessened the scoring burden on him. Sandstrom, however, has speed, quick hands, strong corner skills and an abrasive style that should lighten Gretzky's load in a more direct way.

"Since I got traded away from Edmonton [and from Kurri, the best right wing in the game], I've been the guy going ahead with the puck, waiting for someone [on offense] to jump into the hole," says Gretzky. "Teams had been sending two guys at me. Tomas can carry the puck too, so now, sometimes I can be the guy coming in behind."

Gretzky, who denies having any veto power over Kings trades but is known to have pleaded Nicholls's case against previous trade attempts by McNall and L.A. general manager Rogie Vachon, helped Sandstrom get 18 points in his first 13 games in Los Angeles.

As for those graybeards, defenseman Larry Robinson, 38,

was struggling so badly that last week he was sent home a day early from a winless four-game road trip. Robinson and defenseman Barry Beck, 32, right wing Dave Taylor, 34, and left wing John Tonelli, 32, can no longer play every night. More disappointing, some younger Kings, such as Mike Krushelnyski and Mikko Makela, will not play at full speed.

Los Angeles's talent is still considerable, though, and the Kings, who were eight points behind the third-place Winnipeg Jets but a comfortable 10 points ahead of the fifth-place Vancouver Canucks at week's end, should have the opportunity to rest key players down the stretch. If Hrudey, who is suffering from a mild form of mononucleosis, regains his health and playing form, which was rendered ineffective by the ailment, the Kings could still be a stick of dynamite to either the Calgary Flames or Edmonton in the first round of the playoffs.

That's because they still have Gretzky.

"All these guys are writing that Gretzky is slipping," he said. "It seems like people root for you to get to the top, and then, when you get there, it's almost like they want to see you fail. People say I have a photographic memory on the ice. I don't, but when I read the papers and listen to TV, I do. I remember everything.

"Last year we were riding a high. But this is more fun. This year, there's some adversity, and of course a lot of the heat is on me. That kind of pressure is the thing I enjoy most."

Lemiuex's injuries allowed Gretzky to reclaim the Art Ross Trophy for the 1989–90 season, though he lost out on the Hart to former teammate Mark Messier. The Kings made the playoffs, losing in the second round to Messier's Oilers.

A GREAT 30TH FOR THE GREAT ONE

BY JAY GREENBERG | JANUARY 28, 1991

*Wayne Gretzky hit the big three-oh, but his game didn't show
any signs of slowing down with age*

(Photograph by Ken Levine/Getty Images)

THE KID TURNS 30 THIS WEEK. "YES, BUT TWO WEEKS AFTER my wife did," Wayne Gretzky says, laughing. See, no crisis there. Gretzky's talent took him away from home at age 14 to play junior hockey and burdened him early with the off-ice responsibilities of a phenom. So it was only in playing hockey that The Kid was ever allowed to be a kid. Even when he was a teenager, Gretzky had to act like a 30-year-old. Now that he is about to reach that age, his payback is being able to escape to the rink and be a kid again.

"I have a lot of youth in me," says Gretzky, "because that's what this game is. You've got to have a ball." So he does. After last season, which brought him personal distractions, physical pain and the first flirtations with mortality in a career of epic achievement, Gretzky is now living more happily ever after than he thought possible.

He has a beautiful wife, actress Janet Jones, whom he has assisted on the two biggest goals of his life – Paulina, 2, and Ty, 6 months. And, like his new house in Beverly Glen, Calif., Gretzky sits atop a hill, not over it. At an age when the careers of most hockey players start downward, Gretzky's is still at its peak.

There is no need to wait for his retirement to declare him the greatest player of all time. None of the big scorers of other eras – Gordie Howe, Maurice Richard, Jean Beliveau, Bobby Hull or Phil Esposito – dwarfed their contemporaries the way Gretzky has his. From the 1980–81 season through 1986–87, Gretzky won the scoring title each year by an average of 66 points. Howe will always be known as Mr. Hockey because of his productivity, consistency and longevity (he played 26 seasons between 1946–47 and 1979–80), but those who watched him in his prime insist he didn't significantly raise his level of play during the playoffs. Bobby Orr, a defenseman, revolutionized his position and was the most naturally gifted and exciting player in the game's history. But a bad knee and early retirement curtailed his accomplishments.

When Gretzky won his ninth Hart Trophy as the NHL's Most Valuable Player two years ago, many observers assumed it would be his last. The Pittsburgh Penguins' Mario Lemieux, who outscored Gretzky in 1987–88 and 1988–89, appeared to be taking his place as the best player in the game before a back injury put his career on hold. Now Gretzky, a center, is emerging again, along with St. Louis Blues right wing Brett Hull and Calgary Flame defenseman Al MacInnis, as a leading contender to win the award. The Kings, leaders in the Smythe Division at week's end, are playing well, and Gretzky, who had 91 points, is on his way to his ninth scoring championship.

The 200-point years (Gretzky had four over five seasons from 1981–82 to 1985–86) are over. Gone, too, may be Gretzky's drive to turn good nights into spectacular ones. Coming into this season, he had scored at least five points in a game 86 times. So far this season, he has done so only twice. "I'm not saying I don't have that killer instinct anymore," he says, "but now I realize when the score is 6–2, the coach needs that time to get other people on the team more involved."

Nevertheless, the consistency for which he most prides himself – Gretzky had been held pointless in only four games this season – is still there. So is his hand speed, which has helped him score more points than anyone else in the hockey history. Gretzky scored 142 points in 73 games last season, which made it the first since his NHL rookie campaign, 1979–80, in which he failed to average more than two points per game. And this year it looks as if he might not reach that benchmark again. However, the slippage in his production from his Edmonton Oiler years (1979–80 through 1987–88) is not attributable to age or attitude but to his supporting cast. It's good in L.A but not as good it was with the Oilers.

Gretzky scored an unthinkable 92 goals in Edmonton in 1981–82, including 50 in first 39 games, with Jari Kurri on his right flank. Kurri, a probable Hall of Famer, had one of the best finishing touches in the game's history. Tomas Sandstrom, Gretzky's right wing now, doesn't quite have Kurri's hands, but he possesses good speed, a hard, sinking shot and a chippy style of play that invites retaliation and opens room for Gretzky. Tony Granato, Gretzky's left wing, can score, and Luc Robitaille, who has averaged 49 goals the last four seasons, converts often when Gretzky sends the puck his way on power play. The Kings have provided Gretzky no shortage of players to whom he could pass. What the Oiler teams that won four Stanley Cups in five years (1984, 1985, 1987 and 1988) had that the Kings don't is Paul Coffey. "Coffey is the best passer from goal line to red line in the history of hockey," says Gretzky of his former Oiler teammate, who currently plays in Pittsburgh.

Now when Gretzky, anticipating that the Kings will take possession of the puck in their end, swings towards center ice, the puck doesn't materialize on his stick as cleanly or as often as it did in his years in Edmonton. Coffey's counterpart in Los Angeles, defenseman Steve Duchesne, is far more creative in the opposition end than he is in his own.

Most of Gretzky's Oiler teams benefited from playing portions of games four skaters against four, a facet that has almost disappeared since the NHL's 1986 ruling that coincidental minor penalties no longer affect the number of players on the ice. Speedy Edmonton was especially effective at using the open ice available in such situations. And scoring has dropped considerably in the NHL, from an average of 8.3 goals per game in 1981–82 to 6.78 so far this year. When all these factors are weighed, it's clear that the Great One is no less great than ever.

On Jan. 5 in Toronto, Gretzky crossed the Maple Leaf blue line and faded left. As two Leafs chased him, Gretzky was aware that Kings winger Bob Kudelski was trailing 30 feet behind the play. Gretzky laid a backhand pass perfectly into the path of Kudelski, who ripped a 30-footer past goaltender Peter Ing.

The next evening in Chicago, Los Angeles, which was leading 2–1, was on the power play when Gretzky, holding the puck at the edge of the circle near the boards in the Blackhawks' end, did something unexpected – he shot. "Teams are playing me to pass," he said afterward. "Tommy

[Webster, the Kings' coach] has told me I have to shoot more to create some room." On this occasion, Gretzky shot essentially to create a rebound, and Chicago goalie Ed Belfour obligingly left one in the slot for the fast-closing Kudelski. So Kudelski scored the insurance goal in a surprising 3–1 victory over the Blackhawks, the team with the league's best record.

As the Kings' team-owned private plane – replete with first-class seats, video monitors and all the shrimp cocktail and pasta a club that had just finished a 4–1 road trip clearly deserved – climbed into the sky 90 minutes later, the consensus was that this had been their best defensive game of the season.

"Obviously, I'm tired right now," Gretzky said as he nursed a beer. "I'm very tired. It was a tough game, and I double-shifted a lot and killed more penalties than I have been.

"If there's a difference between now and five years ago, it's that I have to be careful on an off-day like tomorrow. I'm not a fanatic about conditioning, but I realize I have to do some extra things now, like riding the bike. Nolan Ryan and Carlton Fisk didn't just get up at the age of 39 and say they'd better start working harder so they can play another year. They're still playing because they started working harder at 29. But just about every season, there has been a stretch when I'd get tired. I don't think it's any worse now."

Last season's downtime was caused by more than just fatigue. The Kings' defensive inadequacies doomed them to the league's seventh-worst record, and Gretzky struggled through January and February with a nagging left knee injury. On the evening before last year's All-Star Game in Pittsburgh, Bernie Nicholls, one of Gretzky's friends on the Kings, was traded to the New York Rangers for Sandstrom and Granato. The next morning, Gretzky slept in and missed a workout. That same month, a good friend of his and Janet's from Edmonton, Denise Randon, was told she had leukemia. She died last month.

In March, just as Gretzky was starting to feel like his old self, a cross-check delivered by the New York Islanders' Alan Kerr caused him to have back spasms. He played enough to contribute to the Kings' first-round playoff upset of Calgary, but he was finished after Game 3 of Edmonton's second-round sweep of the Kings. Since then, therapy has cured his back ailment, and a talk with Webster has cleared Gretzky's mind.

When Los Angeles owner Bruce McNall paid Edmonton $15 million, three No. 1 draft choices and two good young players (Jimmy Carson and Martin Gelinas) for Gretzky, Marty McSorley and the since-traded Mike Krushelnyski in August 1988, Gretzky became responsible for making the long-suffering L.A. franchise viable. He admits that last season he was increasingly distracted by that burden. "Everyone has been so nice to me, the last thing I want to do is let anyone down," Gretzky says. "I was thinking about everything, from the practice rink to noticing if we had empty seats at games. Tommy reminded me before the season that it's my job to play. That's taken a lot of pressure off me."

It helped, too, that both Gretzky and the Kings started quickly this season. They have improved their defense, but a shortage of depth and the advancing age of important players like Dave Taylor, 35, and Larry Robinson, 39, still leave them with the same kind of team they've had in the last two playoffs: dangerous but not built for the long haul. However, an owner who spent $15 million for the only player he thought could save hockey in Southern California isn't likely to zipper his wallet if, as expected, upcoming collective-bargaining negotiations give players more freedom of movement. McNall, who shares ownership of 14 racehorses with Gretzky, feels compelled to give the Great One a chance at the only thing Gretzky says he wants from his remaining years in hockey: another Stanley Cup.

He has only one more significant individual mark to chase: Howe's NHL-record 801 career goals. Gretzky, who surpassed Howe's NHL career record of 1,850 points last October, doesn't have much stomach to knock his boyhood idol off the top of another list. "I wish I could stop at 800," says Gretzky, who at week's end had 705 career goals. Of course, he won't. Estimated arrival at number 802? Two-and-a-half years, Gretzky Standard Time. Allowing for a slight slackening of his present scoring pace, he should reach 3,000 points at about the time his $31 million contract expires, at the end of the 1997–98 season.

And then? "I don't know," says Gretzky. "I don't want to be a coach or a general manager. I'll be involved with horses. I'll benefit Bruce any way I can and help the league sell the game." McNall predicts that retirement at age 37 will not suit Gretzky if he is still productive. "[Edmonton general manager] Glen Sather says he thinks Wayne will play a lot longer than people think, and I agree with him," McNall says. Janet is certain that whenever her husband's retirement comes, the timing will be correct. "If it seems as if everything in his whole career has been laid out for him," she says, "it's because he knows what's the right thing at the right time. I can't imagine why the end of his career would be any different."

For all he has accomplished, Gretzky remains without pretense and remarkably immune to jealousy on the part of teammates and opponents. His image is absolutely true to his personality. Despite everything he has to be to so many people, he enjoys everything about being Wayne Gretzky. He just likes one part more than the others. "You know how a kid cries if his Little League game is rained out?" says Janet. "That's Wayne. At 4:30 on game day, he starts to sweat a little bit, and he can't wait to go. There is never a time, even last year when things weren't going well, that he dreaded going to a hockey game."

Someday, he *will* retire. And no matter how distant Gretzky is making that time appear, it's not too early to begin dreading it. Though the Kings sell out more nights than not and have surpassed McNall's financial projections, the fan in McNall, more than the owner, finds it disappointing that you can still buy a ticket on almost any game day. "We've done great," McNall says. "But I just think people will look back and realize that they had an opportunity to come and see maybe the greatest sports figure in history – and didn't do it."

Gretzky celebrated his 30th birthday year by collecting 163 points and an Art Ross trophy. This was the last time in his career he topped 150 points in a season.

LOOKING TO A GREAT RECOVERY

BY RICK REILLY | DECEMBER 16, 1991

Wayne Gretzky mulled over retirement after he started slowly and his dad fell gravely ill, but then things got better for both father and son

(Photograph by Bruce Bennett/Getty Images)

WAYNE GRETZKY WAS NOT DEPRESSED. NO. FOR INSTANCE, last month he only thought about quitting hockey twice a day – a.m. and p.m.

"This is the end," he told his wife after another in an assembly line of odorous performances. "This is the end of the end. I never, ever dreamed I could play this bad."

At first his wife, actress Janet Jones, thought he was kidding. So did his coaches. So did former teammate Mark Messier. But Gretzky was serious. "I hate mediocrity," he told Los Angeles Kings assistant coach Cap Raeder. "If there's one thing I can't accept, it's mediocrity."

Actually, "mediocrity" was overdoing it a bit. The way Gretzky was playing, mediocrity was still two floors up. Gretzky was just slightly above horrid and just below rotten. Here it was the 10th game of the season, and he had no goals. Wayne's World without goals? No way! In Canada people checked their calendars to be sure it was hockey season. The Great One had become the Great None. In one 0–4–2 stretch for the Kings in November, Gretzky contributed three whole points. The greatest player in hockey history suddenly couldn't dump a puck into a swimming pool. "I'm the weak link on this team," he told reporters.

Maybe even worse, he had taken the Kings' expensive new foreign import, winger Jari Kurri, and blown his engine. Gretzky's former right wing from the glory days with the Edmonton Oilers had returned from Italy at Gretzky's sincere urging and Kings owner Bruce McNall's sincere $850,000 a year. Talk about steep. To get Kurri, in the off-season the Kings traded their power-play point man, Steve Duchesne, and their best checking center, Steve Kasper. Kurri, who averaged 47 goals a year while playing on Gretzky's line in Edmonton, had a hat trick in the season opener and then scored only two goals in the next nine games. This is the greatest scoring combination of all time? "Maybe we should look at some old tapes," joked Kurri.

All in all, hockey for Gretzky seemed to be one long headache, starting with the day last season when he used his face to stop Duchesne's shot in Game 3 of the Kings' Smythe Division finals loss to Edmonton. Gretzky got 36 stitches and a permanent crease in his left ear by which to remember what he calls "my first blocked shot."

Then, about the time he could hear without having to stand sideways, it was time to play in last summer's Canada Cup. In Game 1 of the best-of-three finals in Montreal on Sept. 14, Gretzky took a dubious shot in his legendarily tender back from Team USA's Gary Suter, who made a run for the border while Gretzky, the eventual tournament MVP, went home crumpled over like Felix Unger.

Then, about the time Gretzky could pick up the morning paper without wincing, it was time to play the NHL exhibition season. He rushed his poor lumbar into action to help his boss fill the outdoor arena at Caesars Palace in Las Vegas for an exhibition game against the New York Rangers.

When your boss is also your business partner in such hobbies as million-dollar racehorses, a Canadian Football League team, priceless baseball cards and precious coins – most of which you know precious little about – you like to keep him happy. But in Vegas, Gretzky got a shove from the Rangers' Mark Hardy in just the wrong part of his back, and it crapped out.

And so it was that Gretzky's back started the regular season in about the same shape that JFK's left the war. By the fourth game the back was less painful, but his game was still hurting. Gretzky was starting to get worried. So he called – who else? – his dad, Walter, affectionately known to him and others as Wally.

"Wally, did you ever think I could play this bad?" he asked glumly from his car phone on the way to practice in L.A.

"Hey, you've had a couple bad games," Wally told him. "But you've had 13 pretty good years, too, don't forget." Wayne allowed himself a small grin at that. The 13 years hadn't been bad, had they? Four Stanley Cups, three Canada Cups, nine Hart Trophies as NHL Most Valuable Player, nine NHL scoring titles, the alltime points and assists records, more money than Croesus. Decent.

Four days later, on Oct. 16, after his fifth straight game without a goal, Gretzky was taking his pregame midday rest at his new Mulholland Estates house when Janet came sprinting into the bedroom with an oh-no look in her eye. "Your sister's on the phone," she said.

THE OLD WALLY GRETZKY WAS A FUNNY LITTLE MAN WITH a size-XL nose and wiry hair that kind of did a Dennis the Menace in the back. He smoked like a 1956 Chevy, a habit he stopped only to sip tea, which he drank by the tankard. He would rarely fall asleep before 2 a.m., partly because he was always talking on the phone and partly because when he stopped talking on the phone, the silence took over and he had to listen to the infernal ringing in his ear that had given him a nice little headache for going on 30 years, ever since he had an accident on his job while repairing underground telephone cable.

Wally didn't have to work. Wayne tried to get him to retire once, but Wally refused. "If I quit," he told Wayne, "how can I tell my kids never to quit?" Wally could live in any mansion he wanted (Wayne once tried to buy him a huge new house), but he stayed in a tiny two-story place on an Archie Bunker kind of block in Brantford, Ont. He could drive any car he liked (Wayne once bought him a brand-new black Cadillac), but he drove an old Chevy station wagon with 180,000 miles on it. He left the Cadillac to others. The Wally policy was never to turn a car in until it had at least 200,000 miles.

In May, Wally, at the age of 53, finally made retirement from Bell Telephone. He had worked his full tour and got his full pension. So here was paradise. And what did Wally do in his retirement? He worked anyway. He began fixing up his late mother's old farmhouse, which Wayne had bought and Wayne's sister, Kim, lives in now, in Cannington, 100 miles from Brantford. It was there, as Wally was repairing a fruit cellar, that the aneurysm in his brain, the one that had been building for years, finally popped.

Wayne chartered a plane, packed Janet, their two kids and his brother Keith in it and flew to Hamilton, Ont., where his father lay at Hamilton General Hospital. Gretzky's father was in intensive care with tubes coming from his head, arms and nose. The doctor warned Gretzky, "He may not make it through the night." But for some reason, Wayne never worried about that: "He still seemed strong to me."

Of course, Wally had always seemed strong to his son. There are fathers and sons who are close, and then there are Wayne and Wally Gretzky, who would talk almost daily about almost anything. Janet could tell you. She learned to stop asking whom Wayne was talking to on the phone. Instead she would say, "How much longer will you be talking to your dad?" Gretzky had always called his dad "my best friend," but now he wasn't entirely sure what his best friend would be like when he woke up.

A delicate operation performed by neurosurgeon Rocco de Villiers three days after Wally's collapse got Wally over the life-or-death part. "He saved my dad's life," says Gretzky. In Canada, Wally Gretzky is sort of the unofficial acting father of hockey, and for De Villiers, saving his life was a kind of healing for the doctor himself. Two months earlier, De Villier's 19-year-old daughter had been kidnapped, raped and murdered in Burlington, Ont., by a man who, the police allege, then killed another woman and committed suicide. "People around the hospital say my dad's situation has given the doctor a boost in the arm," says Gretzky. "It's kind of like God's way of rekindling a fire in this guy."

After missing five games, Wayne rejoined the Kings on Oct. 28. He played a little better, but his production was still way down, and as the Kings pulled into the Bay Area for a game against the San Jose Sharks on Nov. 19, Gretzky had been held pointless in four of his last six games. During that span he scored just one goal.

"Everywhere I went, it became, 'When is Gretzky going to get a goal?'" he said last Thursday. "Here you are, your dad is fighting for his life, and people are coming up to you and asking, 'Are you ever going to score?' And you think to yourself, My goodness."

Gretzky's getting shut out was no longer a UPI flash. It barely made the game notes. He was 30, looking down a long, dark tunnel and seeing only a gold watch. He thought long and hard about taking it and getting on with the next life, driving his kids to dancing lessons, trying to break 80 and being introduced at championship fights. "The whole thing just hit me," he says. "It went from bad to worse, to the point where I had serious conversations with my wife about my career. I hate playing bad. That's my biggest pet peeve.... The last thing I wanted in my career was to not earn my money. And I realized, 'I'm being overpaid out here.'"

The one guy he would have liked to hash it out with, he couldn't. Wally was awake and talking, but he was not quite the same. Once Wayne might have said, "Hey, Wally, we're going to Chicago tomorrow," and Wally might have answered, "Gonna be tough there, very tough game." Now the answer was just, "Oh, that's good."

Wally could remember the past but not the present. He could remember the great games, but not what he had had for breakfast. If, say, Keith visited him in the morning, Wally had no recollection of it an hour later. "It's not really him," says Wayne. "I'd always considered him a very smart man, but now, his common sense isn't there. He's not a very smart man right now.... Here was a man I'd talked with just about every day of my life, and now I don't have that." Gretzky felt a new emptiness.

But what Wayne Gretzky found out is that he had other best friends. "Janet told me, 'You love to play hockey. How can you not play?' And I realized that was the bottom line: I did love it." Then there was Messier, Gretzky's former Oiler teammate who at the time was a new New York Ranger. "He told me, 'The thing that's made you one of the best players over the years has been your mental edge,'" says Gretzky. "'You've just lost it now. You'll get it back. You've got to regroup.'" And finally, there was help from an unlikely source – Raeder, the affable, cupid-faced Kings assistant. "Relax," Raeder told him on Nov. 23. "You don't have to take the whole world on your shoulder. Have fun. Love the game."

One thing about life: You never know who or what is going to rekindle a spark in a man. For some reason this did it, this tip from a former goalie who had never played a single game in the NHL.

"Cap," said Gretzky, as he left the room, "it starts tonight."

And it did. From that night, against San Jose, through last weekend, Gretzky went ballistic – six goals and 15 assists in nine games, including a hat trick. He had points in all nine games and moved from nowhere in the NHL scoring race to sixth and closing fast. To scoring leader Kevin Stevens of Pittsburgh, it must have been like looking in your rear-view mirror and seeing a 747.

The worm had turned. Suddenly, Gretzky was Midas. The CFL's Toronto Argonauts, the team he owns along with McNall and comedian John Candy, won the Grey Cup. This came a day after Gretzky learned that Golden Pheasant, one of his 16 thoroughbreds, had won the $2.77 million Japan Cup. And there was talk that the Honus Wagner baseball card he and McNall paid $410,000 for last March would someday be worth more than $1 million. The way things were going, Gretzky could have put a quarter in a pay phone and expected 20 to 1.

Unfortunately, the Kings' number still hasn't come up. The team was last seen somewhere below .500, having lost five in a row and having gone 3–6–1 in its last 10 games. In one horrid two-game stretch last week – in which Gretzky had a hand in every Kings goal – the Los Angeles defense gave up 100 shots on goal, 49 to the formerly toothless Sharks and 51 to the grateful Chicago Blackhawks. "It's Murphy's Law around here right now," said Raeder in Chicago.

Part of the Kings' slow start is short health, and part is short tempers. Gretzky, Kurri, goalie Daniel Berthiaume and defensemen Rob Blake, Marty McSorley, Charlie Huddy, Larry Robinson and Jeff Chychrun have all missed serious swatches of games with injuries, though none of them has missed more than their coach, Tom Webster. His 12-game suspension for chucking a stick at referee Kerry Fraser on Nov. 16 meant that including time off for punching a player (last April he took a swipe from the bench at Calgary's Doug Gilmour) and the days he was absent because of an ear infection, he will have missed, by the end of the month, 31 regular-season games in the past two seasons. Add it all up, and he has been around for only three quarters of the Kings' games. He's the Johnny Carson of NHL coaches.

"Good teams are built on adversity," says Gretzky. "We'll see how this team pulls out of this."

Speaking of responding, Wally, thanks to De Villiers, is doing some of that already. Though De Villiers figures it will take six months to a year before the Gretzky family knows whether or not Wally will ever be the same, Wayne got a hint on Nov. 26 after a game in Toronto. He had julienned the Leafs for a goal and three assists in a 5–2 win, then gone directly to his dad's bedside.

"How you doing, Wally? Did you see the game?" Wayne asked.

His dad's face hardly twitched. Then he said, "If you were playing better, you would have had a goal and *four* assists tonight."

It looks like Wally will be all right.

Walter Gretzky recovered from his aneurysm, though not without complications. To this day, he remains an active supporter of Canadian hockey programs. He was awarded the Order of Canada in 2007.

RETURN OF THE KING

BY RICHARD HOFFER | JANUARY 18, 1993

Wayne Gretzky, recovered from a career-threatening injury, got back on the ice and mounted one of the greatest comebacks in all of sport
(Photograph by Harry Scull Jr./Getty Images)

LOS ANGELES WAS LOSING ITS STAR POWER, LOSING THE kind of civic franchise players that makes life worth getting on the freeway for. Magic Johnson left the Lakers, and the city's premier glamour team was taken from show business and restored to the NBA. Then it was feared that Wayne Gretzky had departed from the Kings forever, suddenly reminding everybody in L.A. that hockey was actually a Canadian pastime, a kind of roller derby on ice that, on its own, guaranteed no celebrity sighting grander than Alan Thicke.

Well, the Kings have been saved, sort of. Whereas Magic hoped to come back and couldn't, Gretzky could and did. On Wednesday of last week, skating in his first game of the season after a preseason back injury had threatened the remainder of his career, Gretzky deftly dished out two assists against the Tampa Bay Lightning. Two nights later, in Winnipeg against the Jets, a man who couldn't even lift his children last fall because of the pain in his spine scored two goals. "Who else in the world could come back and do that?" said King coach Barry Melrose.

The Kings, however, won neither of those games, which made them winless in 10 straight. (The streak ended on

Sunday night, when Los Angeles beat the Chicago Blackhawks 5–4 as Gretzky had two more assists.) This is a team that started the season fast, skating to a 19–7–2 record, but has struggled since. Now, the Kings have lost to expansion teams with and without the Great One, and as four previous seasons demonstrated, not even the most elegant skater in NHL history can nudge this team over the hump. But the Kings don't need to win to light up the sport. It's enough that Gretzky, even at 31 and with 14 pro seasons – all of them his best – behind him, is back on the ice. "A guy like that," says teammate Tony Granato, "should go out on his own terms."

That serves history. It also serves hockey: For Friday night's game in Winnipeg, where the temperature was – 28°, Gretzky drew a crowd of 14,000 people who apparently had access to extraordinarily reliable car batteries. That's 1,000 more fans than the Kings had drawn on visits here without him in balmier times earlier this season. And an upright Gretzky certainly serves Los Angeles. Last Wednesday, for his return to the Forum, a sellout crowd assembled to adore him. Just to see that familiar number 99, just to see him glide on the ice again, nonchalantly resting one skate atop the other the way he does, was reassuring. To see him circling the net during the game, handling the puck in a manner that mystifies even his coach, serving it up for easy goals, justified all the attention. WAYNE'S BACK! read a hand-lettered sign, articulating a city's excitement, and its relief.

About Wayne's back: The actual ailment is a herniated thoracic disk that radiates pain to his chest. The injury is most likely the result of his getting hit from behind for 14 seasons, a violence that has seemed to escalate against

Gretzky in recent years. And though he had complained of rib pain after last season's playoffs, the cause went undiagnosed. Not until preseason camp, to which he reported in peak condition, did Gretzky experience the excruciating chest pain. Actually, he had no pain through three days of skating. Then he returned home to be with his wife, Janet Jones, as the birth of their third child neared. At home, in the middle of the night, the pain struck, forcing him to the hospital for a week. It was an alarming event all around. "We visited him in the hospital," recalls Granato, "and everyone became as scared as he was."

Doctors knew of no other athlete who had recovered from a herniated thoracic disk to play again. "We have no timetable for this program and will not speculate on a date for his return," said Dr. Robert Watkins, an orthopedic consultant.

Gretzky's gloom was kept fairly secret until Nov. 7, when the TV program *Hockey Night in Canada* broadcast an interview with him. Gretzky looked drained and sounded depressed. It was pretty clear to anyone who saw him: This guy wasn't coming back.

"You have to understand," Gretzky says now, trying to explain the depth of his despair, "this has been my life since I was six." Suddenly it appeared that that life was over. The pain persisted through mid-November, and Gretzky could not imagine returning to play as long as he endured it. But a week or so after that television interview, medical treatment began to reduce the swelling of the disk, and the pain subsided. "The day the pain stopped," Gretzky says, "is the day I became determined to come back."

The determination was double any he had ever shown.

He was not frightened by doctors' warnings that further injury could prove crippling. What scared him was the thought of never playing again. "I was scared by how much I missed it," he says. "I was scared by how much I wanted to play."

Gretzky, the league's alltime points leader, had long since entered a realm of his own. Yet the most paralyzing potential of his back injury was "that I wouldn't be one of the guys."

By Dec. 7 he was back on the ice. Assistant coach Cap Raeder set up skating drills to supplement Gretzky's back rehabilitation exercises. "He ate it up," Raeder says. Gretzky was on the ice before his teammates practiced, sometimes skated while they practiced and was still on the ice when they finished. "He came determined every day, with a purpose every day," says Raeder. "It was like he was desperate, like he found out how much he missed it."

By Dec. 26, Gretzky was practicing with the Kings. He was pain-free, and aerobic tests showed him to be even fitter than he had been for preseason camp. His doctors, who had originally forecast a return to action in March, agreed to a mid-January debut. There was no reason to keep him out any longer.

By the time Gretzky made his first appearance, he had no apprehension about his back. His only concern, it seems, was about looking like an oaf. He had worried aloud that he would somehow mess up, make a fool of himself. He did not. During that first game Melrose watched Gretzky skate behind the net, fetch the puck and blindly feed it to a teammate. Afterward Melrose said, "He doesn't see that guy. I know he doesn't see him, yet he knows that guy is there. You know how they said Ted Williams could see the stitching on the ball? That's how Wayne sees the ice."

This brilliance was reassuring to a city and to a sport. Star-starved Los Angeles – and all of hockey – basked in Gretzky's light, for at least a little while longer.

Gretzky played a career-low 45 games in the 1992–93 season, but despite the injury, still managed a 1.45 point-a-game scoring pace, ending the season with 65 points.

A STAR IS REBORN

BY E.M. SWIFT | MAY 17, 1993

A waning Wayne Gretzky found new life in the postseason,
leading his Kings all the way to the Stanley Cup final
(Photograph by Mike Powell/Getty Images)

WHAT CHILD WAS THIS, HOISTING THE BLACK-AND-SILVER- clad Los Angeles Kings onto his scrawny shoulders? It must have been an apparition. Wayne Gretzky, skating like the Great One of young? And was this hockey in May? In the City of Angels, where thoughts this time of year usually turn to basketball? The divine number 99, the king of Kings, back atop the list of the NHL's playoff scoring leaders, sporting a follow-me glint in his eye? Could any of this possibly be?

Believe it. Better yet, ask the Calgary Flames or the Vancouver Canucks if it was Gretzky or Memorex who burned them for six goals and 13 assists in the Kings' first 10 postseason games. After suffering through the longest and worst season of his career, the 32-year-old Gretzky, the league's alltime leading scorer, was recharged, rejuvenated and playing like a man whose legs have been born again. Good thing, too, for the run-and-gun Kings are going to need a miracle worker to lead them if they are to continue their improbable march toward Lord Stanley's Cup.

You've heard of playoff hockey? Tight-checking, disciplined, close to the vest? The Kings prefer play*ground* hockey. This team never met a two-on-one it didn't like.

Bucking traditionalist thinking, 36-year-old coach Barry Melrose has had his Kings keep the showtime machine on full throttle in the postseason, the result being a declaration of war on goals-against averages. Through those first 10 playoff games the Kings had scored 50 times – but they had allowed 47 goals.

Says Gretzky, who has had points in nine of the 10 games, "The teams that do the best in the playoffs are the ones that change the least. We can't play like [Toronto Maple Leaf coach] Pat Burns's teams. We have to play like our team. Our attitude is to attack, to be aggressive, to apply pressure."

Unfortunately for long-suffering Los Angeles fans, those who live by the attack, die by the counterattack. On Sunday, with an opportunity to build a three-games-to-one lead over the favored Canucks, the Kings were drubbed 7–2 at the Great Western Forum. The loss returned the home-ice advantage to the Canucks, and the teams went back to Vancouver, where Los Angeles had already won once in the series. "It would have made life simpler if we'd won," said Gretzky, who missed on a breakaway but assisted on both of L.A.'s goals in Sunday's defeat. "But we're in the same position now that we were in against Calgary. We've shown that we can win on the road."

The entire hockey world – O.K., except Flame and Canuck fans – has been thrilled by Gretzky's resurgence. Overshadowed in recent years by the Pittsburgh Penguins' Mario Lemieux, Gretzky has become the marquee name that hockey forgot. A career-threatening herniated thoracic disc sidelined him for the first 39 games of the season, and after Gretzky rushed himself back into the lineup in

January, he was no longer hockey's Superman. Instead, he skated like someone was standing on his cape.

In his first 18 games back Gretzky got only 19 points, less than half the 2.265 points-per-game average he had maintained in his 13-year NHL career. He finished the regular season with 65 points in 45 games, the first time that Gretzky had ever failed to accumulate at least 100 points in a season. In one dismal stretch he went 16 games without scoring a goal, seven games more than in any of his previous droughts. This from a man who had *averaged* more than 50 goals a season for his career.

"Maybe I came back a month earlier than I should have," says Gretzky, "but the whole reason for returning as quickly as I did was so that I could be the best that I could be in April. And I played pretty well in the last 25 games. But without the support of the coaching staff and my wife, I might have done something drastic in February."

More troubling than Gretzky's lack of point production was that his return seemed to hurt the team. Led by Gretzky's onetime Edmonton Oiler linemate Jari Kurri, L.A. went 20–14–5 in the games Gretzky missed. But when the Average One came back, the Kings played sub-.500 hockey (19–21–5) for the remainder of the regular season. Kurri, who had accumulated 58 points pre-Gretzky, had his ice time slashed and totaled exactly half as many points in the final 45 games.

Melrose, who's in his first year as coach, attributed the Kings' slump to injuries – forwards Dave Taylor, Tomas Sandstrom and Corey Millen missed a total of 121 games this season – but the nagging suspicion around the league was that the greatest scorer the sport has known had finally been neutralized by a relentless checker called Age. Gretzky no longer could lift his teammates to a higher level.

Which is why very few people gave Los Angeles, which finished third in the Smythe Division, much chance of getting past the second-place Calgary Flames in the first round of the playoffs. In the four seasons since Gretzky was traded to L.A. from Edmonton, the Kings have never advanced beyond the division finals, and this season the prevailing wisdom has been that their style under Melrose is all wrong for postseason play. The Kings, led by Luc Robitaille's 63 goals, boasted the NHL's fifth-best offense, with 338 goals, but they were saddled with the fourth-worst defense, having allowed 340. The 114 power-play goals scored against Los Angeles was the most in team history.

"So what?" said Melrose last week. "The Blackhawks had the best goals-against average in the league, and where are they now? [Chicago was swept in the first round by the St. Louis Blues.] People make too big a deal over the regular season. You don't win Stanley Cups in the regular season."

"A lot of people had written us off," says defenseman Charlie Huddy, a member of five Stanley Cup champions in Edmonton before Los Angeles acquired him before the start of last season. "We just decided, let's go prove every-one wrong. It gives you a little extra incentive when people are putting you down."

The Kings surprised the Flames in a wide-open first-round meeting, winning four games to two in a series that left hockey fans scratching their heads, wondering how the Australian Rules Football scores kept creeping into their morning newspapers. The Kings dropped the second game

9–4 but squeezed out victories in Games 5 and 6 by margins of 9–4 and 9–6, respectively. "Where is it written you have to win with defense?" says Melrose, a trifle, er, defensively. "We have a lot of weapons, and we're a much better team when we play an up-tempo game."

Gretzky missed most of the first game of the playoffs with sore ribs after being cross-checked by Calgary's Joel Otto. He played the second and third wearing a flak jacket, but when his ribs started feeling better – they were reported to be cracked, although they still haven't been X-rayed – Gretzky left the flak jacket off and had a painkiller injected after pregame warmups.

He played as if he had been taken off a leash. Buzzing all over the ice in his familiar bent-over skating style, Gretzky had seven points in the final two games against Calgary, playing, by his own estimation, his best hockey since the 1991 Canada Cup. "Wayne's finally got his conditioning where it should be," says Melrose. "The way he's playing right now. I can put him with anyone, and I've been double-shifting him a lot. It's hard to keep him off the ice."

In the Kings' opening game against the Canucks, one of the biggest teams in the NHL and one that had defeated Los Angeles seven times in nine tries during the regular season, the speedy L.A. forwards were manhandled, and Vancouver won 5–2. But, led by Gretzky's goal and two assists, the Kings squared the series in Game 2 with a 6–3 victory. Gretzky was everywhere, deep in his own zone breaking up Canuck scoring chances, camped behind the Vancouver net, a spot Gretzky refers to as his "office." He sprung Kurri for a shorthanded goal, played on the power play, drew penalties and was the first guy Melrose turned to in four-on-four situations. Once, Gretzky even retrieved goaltender Kelly Hrudey's stick when Hrudey dropped it during a flurry.

"The older you get, the better you understand how important it is to be defensive in your own zone," says Gretzky, who'll never be a candidate for the Selke Trophy as the top defensive forward in the league. "I don't gamble as much as I used to. But I'll tell you what, it's a lot easier to be a defensive player than an offensive one. Anyone who says otherwise is full of it."

"That second game in Vancouver is as good as I've ever seen him play," says Huddy, who saw Gretzky play plenty in their eight years together with the Oilers. "The fire was in his eyes. When he stops, cuts back and accelerates into the holes, he still has that jump in his legs. That part of his game is as quick as it ever was."

Gretzky thinks so, too, though from above ice level he appears to have lost a step from his prime. "You age, but I was never a quick skater," Gretzky says. "The game's faster now. The big defensemen can all skate. I don't think I've gotten slower."

He still operates from the edges of the action – behind the net, along the boards, weaving at center ice – where it is easier to get the puck to him. He then creates his havoc from those spots. However, in a concession to his years, he seldom drives to the net with abandon, which has led to a drop-off in his goal production.

In Game 3 against the Canucks, however, Gretzky scored his 100th and 101st playoff goals – extending his own record – in a 7–4 King win. That victory came in suddenly hockey-mad Los Angeles, where the town's sycophantic celebs were now scrambling to press flesh inside the Kings' dressing room. Gretzky scored once on a two-on-one and once into an open net.

The game's No. 1 star, though, was the 32-year-old Kurri, who scored his fourth goal of the postseason (and 97th of his playoff career) by blowing past Vancouver defenseman Gerald Diduck and roofing the puck over goalie Kirk McLean. Kurri looked as if he were 22 again. "Jari's like a goalie who never makes the tough saves look difficult," said Gretzky. "He's got to be up there with [Toronto center] Doug Gilmour as the best two-way player in the game."

Gretzky, for his part, has come around to thinking that the 39 games he missed may have been a blessing in disguise. "Mentally, it may have been the best thing that could have happened to me," he says. "I'd played so much hockey in my career that it gave me a chance to recharge my batteries. I found that I missed the game. Not just the hockey – everything. The traveling, the dressing room, the people, the peaks and valleys. And it was good for my teammates, too. They got to gain their own identity, gain confidence in each other and themselves. I learned a long time ago that one person can't win a championship in sports. But you can feed off each other."

When Gretzky joined the Kings, he said he had two goals: to help sell hockey in Southern California and to bring the area its first Stanley Cup. He has achieved the first goal, and while he still has a long way to go to reach the second, he's closer now than he has ever been before. Close enough, at least, to dream about the possibility of facing Lemieux in the Stanley Cup finals. "I'd love to go head-to-head against him," Gretzky says. "Like I loved to watch Bird and

Magic in the NBA playoffs. That's what sports are about. He'll be ready. I'll be ready. Because, you know" – the Great One gets that glint in his eye as he says this – "I can still *play* this game."

The Kings finished off the Canucks four games to two en route to a conference final showdown with Doug Gilmour's Toronto Maple Leafs.

KING OF THE KINGS

BY JON SCHER | JUNE 7, 1993

Wayne Gretzky extended his reign as the Great One by leading L.A. past his hometown Maple Leafs to the NHL finals

(Photograph by Bruce Bennett/Getty Images)

IN A STEAMY PASSAGEWAY BENEATH THE STANDS AT Maple Leaf Gardens, Wayne Gretzky brushed the sweat from his famous forehead, took a swig of beer and allowed himself a moment to gloat. It may not have been the greatest night of his life, but it was close. The Los Angeles Kings would be playing in June, and for the first time in a long time, all was right with Wayne's world.

"I don't think I've ever had as much personal satisfaction," Gretzky said last Saturday night, after his three goals and an assist had lifted the Kings to a 5–4 win over the Toronto Maple Leafs in the seventh game of the Campbell Conference finals. "When you're Wayne Gretzky, you take the roses that are thrown at you, but you've also got to take the heat. Well, I took the heat, and I answered the bell."

This is Gretzky's sixth trip to the Stanley Cup finals, but the first for Los Angeles in the franchise's 26-year history. Gretzky played on four Cup-winning teams as an Edmonton Oiler before he was traded to the Kings in 1988, but his California sojourn has been one of promise unfulfilled. It seemed as though it would remain that way forever. A herniated thoracic disk kept him sidelined for L.A.'s first

39 games this season, and his teammates feared that the leading scorer in NHL history was through at 32.

But the back got better, and, baby, Gretzky came back, scoring 16 goals and assisting on 49 others in 45 regular-season games. Most important, he was playing his best hockey as the playoffs neared. So were the Kings, who came together at just the right time for their first-year coach, Barry Melrose. They finished third in the Smythe Division and then knocked off the second-place Calgary Flames and the first-place Vancouver Canucks to advance to the conference finals for the first time since 1969.

"Barry made it clear from the first day of training camp that getting to the playoffs and losing in the first or second round, like the Kings always seem to do, was not what he had in mind," says goaltender Kelly Hrudey, who has redeemed himself with an excellent postseason. "Nobody has ever put this kind of pressure on us."

"Pressure?" says Gretzky, with a smile as wide as Lake Ontario. "This isn't pressure. It's fun."

The playoffs have certainly been fun for Gretzky, who last Thursday night scored a power-play goal 1:41 into overtime to give Los Angeles a 5–4 victory that tied the series at three games apiece. Afterward, Melrose stood a few feet from Goldie Hawn in the Kings' celebrity-filled dressing room at the Great Western Forum and practically guaranteed that his team would advance to face the Montreal Canadiens in the Cup finals.

"We're going to Montreal," Melrose said. Then he repeated it. Twice.

Asked if he was worried that the Leafs might post the quote on their bulletin board, Melrose scoffed. "I may be wrong," he said, "but I don't think a bulletin board has ever won a Stanley Cup."

Neither has a team with a coach who wears his 'do spiky on top and shoulder-length in the back. "He spends more time on his hair than I do," says Melrose's equally flamboyant wife, Cindy, who harangued Canadian television commentator Don Cherry after Game 6 for what she considered unflattering remarks about her husband. She also held up a sign outside the broadcast booth that read, SOUR GRAPES. "She's like Tammy Wynette," an admiring Cherry later told his audience on *Hockey Night in Canada*. "She stands by her man."

Melrose, a 36-year-old former defenseman who spent two seasons as a player with the Maple Leafs, knows how to take care of himself. During Game 1, after Los Angeles defenseman Marty McSorley had laid out center Doug Gilmour, Toronto's best player, with a punishing check, Maple Leaf coach Pat Burns had to be restrained from rushing the King bench. Melrose egged him on by puffing out his cheeks in an impression of his corpulent counterpart. "Get a ——— haircut!" was Burns's weak comeback.

Melrose, instead, cut off criticism of his team – which had played miserably in a 4–1 loss in Game 1 – by taking most of the heat upon himself. That was a good move, like most of the others that Melrose has made. Says Gretzky, "I think I play for the best coach in hockey."

He may be right. Especially when you consider how Melrose has handled the Kings' scary goaltending situation. Hrudey, who wears a samurai headband on the ice, struggled so terribly in midseason that he was replaced first with a rookie, Robb Stauber, and then, more embarrassing, with a 33-year-old minor league journeyman, Rick Knickle, who had never before played in an NHL game. "This was my most frustrating season," says the 32-year-old Hrudey, who finally worked his way back into the lineup when the other goalies faltered. "I knew I had it in me. The biggest obstacle was trying to get the respect back from my teammates."

Gretzky never lost his teammates' admiration, but they seem to have rediscovered their sense of awe. "That was one of the best games I've ever seen him play," said forward Luc Robitaille after Saturday's hat trick. Added defenseman Alexei Zhitnik, "Unbelievable. There's no one like Gretz."

In abandoning the modesty that has been his trademark for most of his 14-year NHL career, Gretzky has embraced the confidence and nonchalance the Kings have exuded in this postseason. It's the same sort of confidence the Los Angeles Raiders made fashionable in their NFL heyday. It's only bragging if you can't back it up, and at week's end the Kings were backing it up with authority.

"It took five years of hard work for me to win a championship with Edmonton," Gretzky says. "This is my fifth year with the Kings. Maybe it's our time."

The Kings faced the Canadiens in the final, winning the first game in Montreal. A bad penalty in the second game led to a Canadiens victory, shifting the momentum in favor of the Habs, who won all the remaining games. The 1992–93 playoffs remain the Kings' last appearance in the Stanley Cup final.

THE GREATEST, AND HOWE!

BY AUSTIN MURPHY | MARCH 14, 1994

Wayne Gretzky was close to surpassing Gordie Howe
as the NHL's alltime goal scorer and solidifying his
position as the greatest hockey player ever
(Photograph by Al Bello/Getty Images)

DRIVING THROUGH THE BLACK ALBERTA NIGHT, MIKE Barnett let his curiosity get the best of him. "You scored on the short side, but there *was* no short side," Barnett, a player agent, said to his client and passenger, Wayne Gretzky.

That was the winter of 1985 or 1986, Barnett recalls, back when the Great One was also the Yellow One when it came to air travel. So Glen Sather, coach of the Edmonton Oilers, would let Gretzky drive the 180 miles to and from Calgary for games against the Flames. It was on the return leg one night that Gretzky found himself being grilled by his driver.

Earlier that evening, as Gretzky cocked his stick for a slap shot from 20 feet, Flame goalie Reggie Lemelin hugged one of the pipes, presumably taking away the short side. Yet that was precisely where Gretzky had put the puck for a goal.

"How did you do it?" Barnett asked.

"Well," replied Gretzky, "I had to turn the puck on its side."

Eight or so years later Barnett is asked, Was he serious?

"*I* wasn't going to ask him," says Barnett.

When you are on your way to becoming the most prolific goal scorer in NHL history, you get the benefit of the doubt.

Hockey's most celebrated player, however, did not begin his NHL career auspiciously. Nearly three full games into his first season, 1979–80, the alleged prodigy from Brantford, Ont., had yet to score a goal. Then, with two minutes to play in a game against Vancouver, Stan Smyl of the Canucks took a tripping penalty. On the ensuing power play, the 18-year-old Gretzky carried the puck out from behind the Vancouver net, faked Canuck goalie Glen Hanlon onto his back and roofed goal number 1.

Final score: 4–4. Date: Oct. 14, 1979. Says Gretzky, "I remember thinking, Wow, even if I never play in the NHL again, at least I scored a goal."

Fourteen years and 60 NHL records later, Gretzky is close to bagging the last significant offensive mark not already his. At week's end he needed four goals to eclipse Gordie Howe's NHL record of 801 career goals. It took Mr. Hockey 1,767 NHL games to reach 801; the Great One will catch him in about 1,120. Gretzky's milestone is the hockey equivalent of Hank Aaron surpassing Babe Ruth's home run record...but doing it in roughly two thirds the time. Yet Gretzky has hardly been obsessed in pursuit of Howe's mark.

"I never really said, 'I gotta get two goals tonight,' or 'I gotta score tonight,' or 'I gotta get three,'" says Gretzky, who turned 33 in January and through Sunday had 33 goals and a league-leading 111 points. "I've never ever felt that way."

Gretzky's feat is all the more remarkable when one considers everything he lacks: size, speed, a hard shot – "You could wear driving gloves and catch one of his shots, and it wouldn't hurt," says former NHL goaltender Chico Resch – the ability to finish breakaways, a selfish bone in his body.

Correctly anticipating that he would be asked to reminisce about Gretzky's first goal, Hanlon, now Vancouver's goalie coach, obligingly obtained and reviewed a videotape of it more than a year ago. Why, then, his refusal to return SI's calls? "He's gone over it so many times now," a Canuck spokesperson says, "it's become a sore point."

Certainly Hanlon has nothing to be ashamed of. He gave up a mere dozen goals to Gretzky, putting him 14th on the list of the Great One's most-victimized masked men. The distinction of being 99's most frequently burned netminder is shared by former Canuck Richard (the King) Brodeur and Mike Liut, who played for three NHL teams. Each surrendered 29 goals to Gretzky. This fact comes from the "Wayne Gretzky All Time Goals Overview," a 27-page, single-spaced document recently released by the NHL. It makes some of the most interesting hockey reading since Ken Dryden wrote *The Game*.

The overview informs us that 78 of Gretzky's goals have won games, 178 have come on the power play, 72 with his team a man down. It breaks his goals down by foe (Gretzky has scored 75 goals against the Winnipeg Jets, his favorite opponent) and facilitator. The list of those assisting on Gretzky goals now includes 99 names, ranging from the obvious (Jari Kurri, who has assisted Gretzky 193 times), to the curious (goaltenders have set up 21 of Gretzky's goals) to the obscure: Where have you gone, Brett Callighen (29 assists) and Gord Sherven (1)?

Riffling ahead, we find the Goaltenders Scored Upon section, which tells a tale of serial humiliation. Gretzky has scored on 140 backstops. He has humbled an Astro (Hardy Astrom, twice) and an Espo (Tony Esposito, six times), beaten a Bunny (Larocque, three times) and mauled a mallard (Clint Malarchuk, nine times). He has victimized three Chevys: Alain Chevrier (six times), Tim Cheveldae (four) and Frank Caprice (three). He has dinged Ing (Peter) and Pang (Darren) thrice apiece, while tallying 46 ENGs – empty-net goals.

The goaltenders, of course, sing Gretzky's praises, but his masked victims also draw comfort from reminding themselves of his mortality. "I remember during the 1980 Stanley Cup playoffs, he came down on a breakaway and shot the puck over the glass," says Resell, who played for four NHL teams and allowed Gretzky 10 goals.

"On breakaways, Wayne was not the best," says Liut.

"Far from it," agrees Don Edwards, a netminder for three teams who yielded 18 goals to Gretzky.

"Early in his career he did a lot of talking," says Brodeur. "He had a reputation as a crybaby."

Back then Gretzky could afford to yap a little: He had muscle-bound enforcer Dave Semenko playing on his line. But the six-foot, 170-pound Gretzky also fought his own battles – in a different way. "If a guy ran him, Wayne would embarrass that guy," says Lee Fogolin, the former Oiler who is now in the construction business in Edmonton. "He'd score six or seven points on him. I saw him do it night after night."

On the first day of training camp in 1979, Fogolin, who had been acquired from the Buffalo Sabres in the off-season, asked a member of the Oiler staff to introduce him to this kid everyone was talking about, this Gretzky. "He's in high school," came the reply. "He'll be here for the afternoon practice."

"I'm thinking, This is who they're going to build the team around, a *high school* kid?" says Fogolin. "It took me about two days to see how special he was. This is not an ordinary superstar we're talking about. This is the greatest player ever to put on a pair of skates."

One of the few knocks on Gretzky is that he sometimes overpasses. "I've been criticized by coaches and teammates for not shooting enough," he says. "Maybe they have a point. Goaltenders have fatter pads now than in the early 1980s, which give up more rebounds. And the goal comes off its moorings more easily than it used to, so players can drive to the net harder now to pick up those rebounds. Maybe I'll have to adjust my game a little bit. But I like to think that throughout my career, it's been O.K., playing the way I play, so I haven't really changed my style. Know what I mean?"

Brodeur surely does. That he yielded 29 to 99 seems understandable. As Smythe Division neighbors, the Canucks and Oilers played each other as many as eight times per season. So familiar were these two antagonists, in fact, that they kept up a running dialogue on the ice. "When I made a save against him, I'd say something like 'Not this time!'" recalls Brodeur. "And he'd yell, 'I'll be back!'"

Less comprehensible is the success Gretzky had against Liut, who played for the St. Louis Blues, the Hartford Whalers and the Washington Capitals. "It was luck, more than anything," says Gretzky. "I scored some real lucky goals on Mike – from behind the net, off the face-off. It was just one of those things."

The goals that Liut most vividly remembers Gretzky scoring against him were on Feb. 18, 1981. Liut, then with St. Louis, was still basking in the glow of his MVP performance at the Feb. 10 NHL All-Star Game when he took the ice at the Northlands Coliseum.

"We were down 4–2 going into the third," says Liut, now in his second year of law school in Detroit. "Wayne already had one. About six minutes into the period, Kevin Lowe comes in on a breakaway and dekes me into the back of the net. I make the save, but I'm floundering, and Gretzky scores on the rebound. I put my head down, and I'm thinking, It's O.K., we're still in this thing. But while my head was down, I missed the draw. I look up, and here comes Gretzky on a breakaway. He puts it right through me. Nine seconds, two Gretzky goals. I got the hook."

Into the game skated Eddie Staniowski, who gave up another pair of goals to 99. That night Gretzky became the fifth NHL player ever to score four times in one period. The contest also marked the first of Gretzky's four five-goal games. The next one came 9½ months later in Philadelphia, capping one of the most astonishing scoring sprees in the annals of sports.

Going into the Northlands Coliseum on Dec. 30, 1981, Gretzky had scored 45 goals in his team's first 38 games. "I had never really played well against Philly," says Gretzky. "I did O.K., but I never really lit it up." A fluky first-period goal – an Oiler slap shot from the blue line caromed off the end-boards and back onto Gretzky's stick, allowing him to easily beat Flyer goaltender Pete Peeters – was a hint that Gretzky's fortunes against Philadelphia had changed. "I remember thinking, Wow, this could be a big night," he says.

Gretzky had four goals by the time Flyer coach Pat Quinn, his team trailing 6–5, pulled Peeters with a minute to play in the third period. In the game's final seconds, Oiler wing Glenn Anderson sent Gretzky in on a breakaway, and he scored into an open net. "I remember arguing with Pat Quinn when he pulled me," says Peeters, now a goaltending coach for the Jets. "If Wayne was going to get his 50th, I wanted him to get it against a goalie. But Pat wanted to win."

In the history of the league, only two players, Maurice (the Rocket) Richard of the Montreal Canadiens and Mike Bossy of the New York Islanders, had scored 50 goals in his team's first 50 games of the season. Both had needed all 50 games to do it. In his third NHL season, Gretzky did it in 39.

Was Peeters embarrassed by his role on that historic evening? Hardly. "Wayne got what, five that night? Believe me, it could have been nine or 10. I have vivid memories of coming out, challenging him, stopping him. And he hit at least three pipes. I can still hear them ringing."

After averaging 71.5 goals per season in his first six years in the league – in 1981–82 he scored 92 goals, breaking Phil Esposito's single-season mark of 76 – Gretzky has averaged 42 over his last eight seasons (he missed 39 games in 1992–93 with a herniated disk, finishing with only 16, by far his least productive year). In the second half of his career, he has devoted himself more to setting up goals than to scoring them.

Says Gretzky, "If you sat down and said, 'Name the four best goal scorers in hockey,' my name probably wouldn't come up. My playmaking has probably overshadowed my goal scoring a little bit."

How could it not? He became the NHL's alltime assist leader six years ago. Four times he could have won or tied for the league scoring title on his assists *alone*. In three of those seasons, he also led the league in goals.

"Some guys are just pure goal scorers," says Gretzky. "I don't know if I was a pure goal scorer. I didn't have a very hard shot. I *still* don't have a very hard shot."

What he does have is anticipation bordering on clairvoyance. "I'd direct a rebound into the corner," says Liut, "and he'd be there waiting for it – *bang*, right back at me. It was like he knew where I was going to send the puck before *I* did. How does he do that?"

"What I want to know," says Resch, "is how did he always know what the toughest play would be for the goalie to make? He was always jamming me on my glove side, shoulder high, or putting the puck eight or 10 inches off the ice on my stick side. With Wayne, there were no routine plays. Was he a goaltender once? Did Walter [Gretzky, Wayne's father] teach him that?"

Wayne takes those questions seriously. "I studied the game. I respected everyone I ever played against. And I was ready to play every night."

The night Gretzky breaks his longstanding record is not an occasion that Howe is looking forward to. He has decided not to be on hand when Gretzky erases his mark, and he reminds people of the 174 goals he scored in six World Hockey Association seasons. "Don't confuse people," Howe recently instructed *The Hockey News*. "Eight hundred one is an NHL record. The career [record], he has a little way to go."

Will Gretzky, who has 46 WHA goals himself, stick around long enough to claim Howe's career mark?

"I'm not ruling it out," he said on a rainy afternoon in San Jose last month, two hours before facing the Sharks. "I just plug along. The game still brings me joy. Like last night, when [King defenseman-forward] Marty McSorley scored in the first 20 seconds." In his first shift since being traded back to L.A., McSorley got one off a Gretzky feed. As they embraced, Gretzky's smile lit up the Forum.

"Moments like that are more exciting for me now than they were 10 years ago," says Gretzky. "Ten years ago we used to think, This is going to happen every day, we'll do it again tomorrow. Now I really relish those moments."

He excuses himself to get dressed. The best player ever to put on skates still has a few such moments in him.

Just over a week after this article was on newsstands, Gretzky surpassed Howe's NHL goal record, scoring his 802nd goal against Kirk McLean of the Vancouver Canucks.

LESS THAN GREAT

BY MICHAEL FARBER | MARCH 6, 1995

Wayne Gretzky was having a subpar year and feeling heat over trades made by the Los Angeles Kings

WAYNE GRETZKY, UNSHAVED AND UNAPOLOGETIC, STOOD
in a dim light outside the Los Angeles Kings' dressing room last week and addressed the question, Is this the twilight of a god?

The prospect that it is might haunt the NHL, which has not produced any other stars who are bankable in the U.S., but it is not haunting Gretzky. Gretzky never has tried to kid himself. He knows the end is out there somewhere. Some days it seems distant, other days it's as close as a mirror.

In the first third of this season, the Great One has been easier to find in the athletic actuarial tables than among the NHL's scoring leaders. Gretzky, who won last season's scoring title with 130 points and has averaged 2.17 points per game in 15 NHL seasons, had four goals and 17 points in 17 games through Sunday. A point a game is acceptable for almost everyone except Gretzky. But the King center had just two even-strength goals, and his minus–14 was the worst plus/minus rating among NHL forwards, which is acceptable for no one. The slump would be an insignificant blip but for one thing: Gretzky turned 34 on Jan. 26. The day he retires, which is the day every team should haul 99 to its rafters because no NHLer should ever again be allowed to wear that number, is no longer somewhere over the rainbow, although Gretzky isn't ready to slip into his anecdotage, a lifetime of banquet speeches detailing hockey's most fabulous career.

"I'd be lying if I didn't stand here and say, yeah, there are nights when I don't know if I am near the end," Gretzky says. "Am I a different player? Has the way I play and the style of my game deteriorated that much in six months? I'll have to fight through it. I'll have to work to a point, give it my best effort, and if I come up short, I'll have to figure out what the next stage of my career is."

He might want to pass on, say, becoming a general manager. Gretzky certainly wasn't the triggerman, but the police are dusting for his fingerprints on the puzzling, three-for-three deal on Feb. 14 with the Buffalo Sabres that brought to the Kings 32-year-old goalie Grant Fuhr, who helped Gretzky's Edmonton Oilers win four Stanley Cups in the 1980s, and unproven young defensemen Philippe Boucher and Denis Tsygurov. The cost was a potential star defenseman, Alex Zhitnik, veteran defenseman Charlie Huddy and backup goalie Robb Stauber. Zhitnik, 22, broke his left thumb in his second game with the Sabres but is expected back soon.

The acquisition of Fuhr, who becomes an unrestricted free agent on July 1, appears to be a huge no-confidence vote for streaky King veteran Kelly Hrudey, whose respectable 2.83 goals-against average and .921 save percentage make him seem more like a solution than a problem for a team in 10th place (5–8–4) in the Western Conference at week's end. "Ridiculous," says one Eastern Conference general manager of the deal. "You trade for Fuhr if you think you can make a run at the Stanley Cup, but the Kings are a long way from that. They're going to have a tough time making the playoffs."

Whenever the Kings acquire an ex-Oiler – seven teammates from Edmonton's Stanley Cup years have joined Gretzky since he was traded to Los Angeles in 1988 – or some other FOG (Friend of Gretzky), the world looks for the unseen hand. On XTRA, the all-sports station that broadcasts King games, irate callers leveled charges of cronyism at Gretzky and mourned the loss of Zhitnik, the latest in a line of prominent rushing defensemen (others include Larry Murphy, Garry Galley and Paul Coffey) that the Kings have exiled the past 12 years; two blasphemers even said that Gretzky must go. The score on the trade on *The Los Angeles Times* letter page was Sabres 7, Kings 0.

"The assumptions are this was a Fuhr-for-Zhitnik trade and that Gretzky made the deal," says Sam McMaster, the Kings' rookie general manager. "Wrong. This wasn't Zhitnik for Fuhr. We got two really good young prospects, a first-rounder [Boucher in 1991] and a first pick [Tsygurov, No. 38 overall in 1993]. We're trying to win now, but we're also trying to build for the future. And the Los Angeles Kings made the deal – the coaching staff, the scouts and me. If we're right, god bless us, and if we're wrong, we'll carry on. Wayne found out after the players we traded."

If Gretzky didn't have his prints on the deal, he does have his imprint on McMaster. Gretzky has known McMaster since Gretzky was 14 and playing for McMaster's Toronto Young Nationals junior B organization. Gretzky recommended McMaster, among others, as a candidate to succeed former general manager Nick Beverley, who had clashed with coach Barry Melrose and had a cool relationship with Gretzky and some of the other players. "I'm not sensitive about that – I'm proud," says McMaster, an avuncular 50-year-old who ran the Sudbury Wolves of the Ontario Hockey League for the past six seasons. "I would have never been hired in L.A. if Wayne hadn't brought my name up, but everybody has to have an in in this business. If one of the greatest hockey persons of all time recommends me and that's a reason I'm here, that's an honor."

McMaster did ask Gretzky for an assessment of Fuhr when he played in Europe on Gretzky's touring team during the lockout; Gretzky said Fuhr played "marvelously." "Now we have to get Grant back to playing shape," McMaster says. Fuhr, who had been buried in Buffalo behind Dominik Hasek, allowed nine goals (seven on power plays) against the Vancouver Canucks in his first four periods as a King.

You can't say the lunatic is running the asylum, since Gretzky always has represented himself and hockey with grace. So let's put it this way: The icon has helped run the sacristy. As befits a legend who made hockey work in California and helped establish the NHL's popularity in other nontraditional hockey venues, his influence on the Kings has been enormous since Day One. Even before Day One. Gretzky sat in former owner Bruce McNall's office giving hand signals as McNall hashed out details of the pending Gretzky trade on a speaker phone with Oiler owner Peter Pocklington. Gretzky asked McNall not to close the deal without landing tough-guy defenseman Marty McSorley as part of it, which he did.

Gretzky as G.M.-without-portfolio became an NHL inside joke. Even the Kings laughed about it. At the 1992 press conference when McNall promoted Beverley to G.M., McNall said, "O.K., Wayne, take off that Nick Beverley mask."

Gretzky and McNall were close. McNall, who is expected to be sentenced in July after pleading guilty on Dec. 14 to two counts of bank fraud, one count of wire fraud and one count of conspiracy in connection with allegedly inflating his net worth and whose remaining 28% of the team is being held by a bankruptcy trustee, didn't just trade for a player when he acquired Gretzky. He made an investment. Gretzky's salary – he is in the second year of a three-year, $25.5 million deal – made him more like a partner than an employee. In fact, he became partners with McNall in ownership of the Toronto Argonauts of the Canadian Football League, some racehorses and a 1910 Honus Wagner baseball card purchased for $451,000 in 1991. "Bruce had a unique relationship with Wayne," says Roy Mlakar, the former King president who resigned in April and is now the Pittsburgh Penguins' CEO. "A name of a player would come up, and Bruce would say, 'Oh, Wayne likes that guy.' You can't underplay that close a relationship, but Wayne was a huge asset while I was in L.A."

Beverley, now the director of scouting and player personnel for the Toronto Maple Leafs, is guarded on the subject of Gretzky. "There was an element of discomfort because of the relationship between ownership and Gretzky that didn't sit well in the dressing room," says Beverley, who traded Coffey, one of Gretzky's best friends, to the Detroit Red Wings in January 1993, and forward Tomas Sandstrom to the Penguins in February 1994. Current King players dispute Beverley's contention that Gretzky's power created tension on the club, although the relationship between Gretzky and former star left wing Luc Robitaille did grow strained. When McMaster traded him to Pittsburgh for rightwinger Rick Tocchet on July 29 – one of the rare King deals in recent times that hasn't backfired – Robitaille spoke out. He didn't use Gretzky's name, but he said, "Players should play, and managers should manage. Maybe one of the reasons I'm going is because I agree with that."

"I used to worry about that," Gretzky says of the perception that he is a player-general manager. "If we traded for an ex-Oiler, people would say, 'Oh, wow, that's Wayne Gretzky's deal.' That bothered me tremendously. Then I saw Mark Messier [his former Edmonton teammate and a current New York Ranger] skating with the Cup with about six ex-Oilers around him, and now I don't give a flying — . With an opportunity left to win a Cup, I don't care who's on my side."

That window of opportunity looks grimy. Since losing in the 1993 Cup finals to the Montreal Canadiens, Los Angeles has won only 32 of 101 games. The Kings are in transition. They are bigger, tougher and marginally more conscientious on defense than they were last season, but right now they are no better. Their defense has been eviscerated by injuries, forcing the team to play youngsters. The peach-fuzz blue line has undermined Gretzky's offense more than his increased defensive responsibilities have, because his great asset always has been an ability to exploit his options. This season he has not been receiving crisp breakout passes from the King zone nor has he had trailing defensemen who can do something with his drop passes at the other end of the ice.

But Gretzky makes no excuses. He never has. "I only compare myself to myself," he says, "and when I've been mentally strong, I've been dominating. Mentally I haven't been strong enough. If I'm contributing what I should, we could have won some of the games we didn't."

Age isn't an ally of Gretzky's, but don't count him out yet. In February 1993, buried in a career-worst streak of 16 games without a goal after having missed 39 games with a herniated thoracic disk, he moped through All-Star weekend in Montreal. Four months later, on top of his game, he was back in the Montreal Forum playing in the Stanley Cup finals.

"Wayne has played more hockey than almost anyone in the world, a hundred games a year, so age is a factor," Melrose says. "For periods he can still be the best player in the world. He has to find the fire because we're not going anywhere without Wayne Gretzky."

And Gretzky isn't going anywhere without the Kings. There has been speculation that if the Kings don't right themselves, next season Gretzky would be willing to move to a contender unafraid of his hefty contract – the Red Wings, maybe? – and try for a fifth and farewell Stanley Cup. Gretzky says no. "My life is in L.A.," he says. "I will end my career as an L.A. King. I've spent count-less hours, not only in the dressing room, but selling the sport and promoting the NHL. I don't have the desire or the energy to start all over again. It's a big commitment to go to another organization. This is it. When it's over here, it's over."

Kings' coach Barry Melrose was fired halfway through the 1994–95 season, but the change did nothing to right the ship. Gretzky's point production slowed that season to a point a game, and L.A. missed the playoffs. Despite assurances he would finish his career a King, Gretzky was traded the following season.

KING NO MORE

BY RICHARD HOFFER | MARCH 11, 1996

*By forcing Los Angeles to trade him, Wayne Gretzky escaped
a losing team – but he also tarnished his image*
(Photograph by Bruce Bennett/Getty Images)

IT WAS AN ODD LITTLE ERA, AS REMARKABLE FOR THE things that didn't happen as for the things that did. The Gretzky years? All the Los Angeles Kings got out of them were increased ticket prices (choicest seats rose from $17.50 to $90), a much needed revenue stream from expansion fees (thanks to Gretzky, a regional sport became national in the 1990s as teams were added in San Jose, Tampa Bay, Miami and Anaheim) and, despite all that, bankruptcy. It was not that much of a success story when you think about it. A good idea going in – star-driven Los Angeles trades for the greatest star in hockey – but not so brilliant coming out. After 7½ seasons together the Kings were again well under .500, attendance was in decline, and Wayne Gretzky, hockey's most important resource, was distracted, miserable and 35 years old. And in all that time the Kings didn't win a Stanley Cup. That's the main thing that didn't happen.

There was some excitement, no question. In California, Gretzky conferred glamour and legitimacy on a sport that had been basically a cult activity. His legacy will out-live his playing days as long as kids clamor for ice time at local rinks. But, really, the whole experiment was a wash professionally, and now that it's over, everybody seems a little worse off for having participated in it. As a fresh, slightly less anticipated era begins in St. Louis, where Gretzky resumes his career with the Blues, the Kings and Gretzky struggle to recover dignity and reputation. If the Gretzky era didn't end in outright disaster, it certainly finished with more disappointment than his legend would seem to have allowed.

The Kings, of course, will be a long time recovering. Despite their appearance in the Stanley Cup finals three years ago, when they lost to the Montreal Canadiens in five games, the club is in disrepair. The owner who brought Gretzky to L.A., Bruce McNall, filed for bankruptcy in May 1994, sold the Kings that spring and awaits sentencing after pleading guilty to fraud and conspiracy charges in connection with the operation of several of his businesses. The team's new owners, Philip Anschutz and Edward Roski Jr., are committed to a rebuilding process, which Los Angeles fans do not usually suffer gladly. The three players who arrived from St. Louis last week (along with two draft picks) in the Gretzky trade – forwards Roman Vopat, Craig Johnson and Patrice Tardif – do not suggest that the process will be speedy, either; Vopat is the only blue-chip prospect among them. Regardless of the owners' avowed intentions and supposedly deep pockets, their failure to re-sign Gretzky marks yet one more misfire in a history of poor trades and drafts for the franchise.

But looking even worse than the Kings, who at least have the benefit of time and of fans' eventual amnesia, is

Gretzky, who has been subjected to a surprising backlash and might not play long enough to outlast it. Suddenly the Great One, whose 61 NHL records only partly account for his role as the game's ultimate ambassador, finds himself defending his sense of loyalty and honor and even the remains of his ability.

Questioning Gretzky's ability was one thing; he already has 18 professional seasons under his belt, and he scored just 15 goals in 62 games for the Kings this season. "How much can he really have left?" asked one anonymous hockey executive in Canada's *Financial Post*. "It tells you a lot when you see how many teams didn't even make an offer on him."

But worse, much worse, was the revisionist history being written about one of the most popular athletes of all time. So now he was a *bad* guy? In the days after Gretzky orchestrated his leaving by publicly demanding that the Kings either acquire top-notch talent to make a run at the Cup immediately or trade him, the newspaper columns were lively with quotes from anonymous – always anonymous – general managers who questioned his, uh, team spirit. "Wayne is out for himself and himself only," read one blind quote in Toronto's *Globe and Mail*. And writers all over North America were remembering instances that cast Gretzky – the NHL's alltime assist leader, for goodness' sake – as a selfish and manipulative player.

Manipulative, yes, as any superstar might be these days. When you take a close look at it, all that happened is that Gretzky, who was in the final year of his three-year,

$25.5 million contract with the Kings and was about to become an unrestricted free agent, began examining his options. Depending upon your point of view, he then either held a gun to the Kings' heads or he gave them fair notice of his intent to leave so they might obtain something in a trade.

Barry Melrose, the Kings' coach from 1992 to 1995, who is an analyst with ESPN, thinks it's the latter. "You can't blame Wayne for this," Melrose says. "He's working under rules that were going to make him a free agent. I think this is coming out wrong, and I don't like the slant. The idea that he's a spoiled brat is ridiculous."

Still, that is the idea. In recent weeks Gretzky has been perceived in some quarters as a selfish bully for using his superstar clout and impending free agency to try to mold an immediate winner, at whatever cost, so he could get another Stanley Cup for himself. As Gretzky campaigned to become part of a better team, and as the Kings went further south and his own play declined, it became popular to characterize his year as a kind of holdout, the difference being that he was actually collecting a paycheck.

The league became concerned, watching its star attraction appear on the evening news, looking more and more wan each night as the saga played out. NHL commissioner Gary Bettman admits to being alarmed at the nature of the "public spectacle." At least one nonanonymous general manager concedes developing a certain disappointment in Gretzky as the affair dragged on.

"I know all players today approach the game in a businesslike fashion," says Vancouver Canucks general manager Pat Quinn. "After all, they're dealing with an asset that happens to be themselves. But his strategy seems to have backfired. I'm like the rest of the fans out there. I didn't like what I saw."

The Kings didn't exactly discourage anyone from putting that spin on the situation. During a Kings-Rangers broadcast from Madison Square Garden in January, longtime Kings play-by-play announcer Bob Miller quoted a New York *Daily News* column: "And when the Rangers got swept against the Flyers last spring and looked too old and too slow, [Mark] Messier did not go looking for another contender. He did not look to force a trade or beat a contract." According to the *Los Angeles Times*, Miller did not get around to reading the part of the column that pointed out that Messier had held out and missed training camp in 1994 in an attempt to negotiate a new deal.

The upshot was that Gretzky, playing just 18 minutes a game for a terrible team and resigned to a change, was looking childish. "Why does it seem that the halo has started to tilt?" wrote an *Edmonton Journal* columnist. And a relatively unblemished career was being examined for behavioral pockmarks. Remember after the Kings lost to the Canadiens in the 1993 finals, and in what should have been a celebration of the Cup's 100th anniversary, he hogged the spotlight with his maybe-I'll-retire comment? Notice how he maintains a generous coterie of writers and broadcasters, how he seems to organize trades for friends and former teammates? He is shrewd, well aware (*too* aware, some say) of his accomplishments and his impact on the game. Wouldn't you be if, midway through your career, a former employer – the Edmonton Oilers in this case – erected a statue in your honor? In the hours before his trade was announced to the rest of the world on Feb. 27, Gretzky began dialing up hockey writers on both sides of the border, giving about a dozen of them the pride of a "scoop." A courtesy to old friends (not all of them were old friends, though) or just politicking?

Gretzky admits he's hurt by all this, but in his newfound excitement of playing alongside Brett Hull on the Blues, he hardly appeared defeated by public sentiment. After his first game with the Blues, in which he scored a breakaway goal in a 2–2 tie against Vancouver, he was babbling like a schoolkid, talking about the playoff-like buzz of playing for St. Louis. Hockey was fun again.

"I want to win," he said last Friday, standing outside a practice rink in Vancouver. "To criticize me for stepping forward to complain about mediocrity, well, for people to accept losing in life, that's not right."

Still, Gretzky says he came very close to doing just that, "to taking the comfortable way out." Never mind that the Kings had failed again to upgrade the team in the off-season; he would have re-signed if the club had offered a contract extension as recently as November. He and his wife, Janet, had built a new home on a golf course north of Los Angeles. His kids (Paulina, 7, Ty, 5, and Trevor, 3) were happy in school. Gretzky liked everything about living in the glamour capital of this continent. "I could go into a restaurant," he says, "and I'm the Number 6 celebrity. I wouldn't be bothered." He could have remained an institution, a civic monument fortified by loyalty and history.

However, as the season dragged on, Gretzky began to understand his looming leverage. The Kings were hopeful of signing him; on the day of the trade, they offered him a long-term contract that would have retained him in an executive capacity after he retired. Gretzky could have been a King for life. Yet the team was equally determined to forge ahead with a youth movement. "I might have seen a Stanley Cup as a King," Gretzky says, "but I would have been on the golf course, not the ice."

Meanwhile, the man who ushered in the Gretzky era in Los Angeles wonders if hockey can survive there without the Great One's star power. "This is not Vancouver," McNall says. "The people won't just show up." McNall is sympathetic to the new owners but thinks they might be missing the big picture. After all, Gretzky is the guy who filled the Forum and who assured TV executives and cereal makers that hockey was a coast-to-coast sport. "He changed the face of hockey," McNall says. "Not only by bringing in expansion but by bringing in TV contracts with ESPN and Fox. He was instrumental in making this a major sport."

Gretzky still has his supporters, people who think that he is much more than a marketing icon. And he still has the kind of on-ice charisma to generate interest wherever he goes. He'll have that for a long time, no matter the sniping.

All the same, though, there is that sniping. Unfortunate reservations about his character will haunt one of sport's last good guys, maybe forever. There could be a dawning awareness that over the last 7½ years Gretzky was good for hockey in general but not for the Kings in particular – that he left them no better than when he found them. The end of the Gretzky era, with its attendant ugliness, ought to remind any superstar who would skate effortlessly into history that he should safeguard, really conserve, his reservoir of goodwill. Because he'll need every drop on the way out.

Though Gretzky's point production remained consistent, the expected chemistry with Brett Hull never materialized. The Blues were eliminated in seven games by the Red Wings in the conference semifinals. Gretzky became a free agent in the summer and began entertaining offers.

THE GOOD OLD DAYS

BY E.M. SWIFT | OCTOBER 7, 1996

*That's what Mark Messier and Wayne Gretzky hoped
to recapture in their reunion as New York Rangers*
(Photograph by Bruce Bennett/Getty Images)

"ONE LAST HURRAH?" MARK MESSIER REPEATS, HIS EYE-
brows coming alive with rippling menace, like a pair of
Doberman pinschers straining at the leash. Let us at him,
boss, they growl, arching above the fire of his eyes. With
effort Messier gets those two sleek, dark man-eaters under
control, and they lie down watchfully. "One last hurrah is
not a language I'm speaking," says Messier, the 35-year-old
New York Rangers captain. "Sometimes I feel like I could
play for another 10 years. And there's still only a handful
of guys who can put up the numbers Wayne can. He's skating as well as he has in the last three or four years."

The subject, of course, is New York's off-season free-
agent addition of Messier's golfing partner, the NHL's alltime leading scorer, fella by the name of Gretzky. There was
a time, from 1979–80 to 1987–88, to be precise, when the
one-two punch of Messier and Gretzky – both of whom
play center, one like a bull, one like a matador – wreaked
havoc throughout the league. Teammates for nine seasons
during the glory days of the run-'n'-gun Edmonton Oilers,
possessors of 10 Stanley Cup rings between them, winners
of 11 regular-season MVP awards and three Stanley Cup
MVP trophies, Messier and Gretzky are hockey's version of

Ruth and Gehrig. But time reels everyone in sooner or later, and Gretzky, like Messier, will turn 36 in January. Counting playoff, Canada Cup, World Cup, All-Star, exhibition and regular-season games, these two have logged more ice time in the last 17 years than Canadian Club. Their speed has diminished, if not exactly fled, and injuries (Gretzky's back and Messier's shoulder and wrist) linger ever longer. The Gretz-and-Mess show on Broadway is certain to have irresistible commercial appeal, but how long can it possibly run? "My wife, Janet, asked me if I'd retire after this year if we won a Stanley Cup with the Rangers," Gretzky says. "I told her, 'Nope, I'll try to win another one.'"

Questions about Gretzky's age resurfaced during last month's World Cup. After proving himself Canada's best forward in the opening three rounds of the tournament, Gretzky was rendered largely ineffective by the tighter checking he encountered in the championship round, a best-of-three series that Canada lost to a younger, faster U.S. squad. "The naysayers have doubts about signing older guys," says Rangers general manager Neil Smith, who in July got Gretzky's name on an incentive-laden two-year, $10 million deal. "People wonder whether Wayne and Mark will still have enough gas in their tanks to perform in the playoffs. But these guys know how to win. I'm proud to be the general manager who gave our fans a chance to see Wayne Gretzky in a Rangers uniform, even if it's only for a couple of years. I hope he'll make those people who've been negative about him eat their words."

Never underestimate the rejuvenative powers of revenge. Gretzky, who hasn't had his hands on the Cup since being traded from Edmonton to the Los Angeles Kings in 1988, has a well of pride that's almost as deep as his stack of scoring records is high. Stung by criticism last year that he was more concerned about himself than the Kings, Gretzky is out to prove that old number 99 is still a lot like the number 99 of old. In New York he will have a supporting cast that Los Angeles couldn't surround him with for the past two years: Nine Rangers participated in the World Cup, the most of any NHL team. "Last year was the toughest of my career," Gretzky says. "I told Kings management from Day One that we had to go after two or three quality guys because we weren't good enough to win with what we had. When nothing was done, I felt I owed it to myself to say something. I was at a crossroads of my career."

Before last January's NHL All-Star Game, Gretzky said that if Los Angeles wasn't going to make a major midseason deal that would enable it to compete for the Cup, it should trade him. This ultimatum caught hockey people by surprise. Gretzky was the Kings' captain and biggest draw, and most observers believed that his influence with the L.A. front office – influence he denied having – had contributed greatly to the makeup of the club. After Gretzky made his demand, the anti-Gretzky backlash was swift and unexpectedly widespread, considering his longstanding reputation as a goodwill ambassador for the sport.

"The Kings wanted to rebuild the hockey club," Gretzky says. "It was probably the right move, but no one told me that's what they were doing. So I forced their hand and ended up being portrayed as the bad guy."

When it became clear that the Kings would accommodate Gretzky's wishes and trade him, the Rangers were one of the clubs that pursued a deal for the Great One. Smith had already asked Messier about Gretzky. Smith knew the two players were close, but he wanted to be sure New York's chemistry wouldn't be thrown out of balance if Gretzky joined the Rangers. "Over the years Mark and I had chatted about all the guys he had played with," Smith says, "and Mark had mentioned several times that if I could ever get Wayne, to do everything I could to do it. But we weren't going to give up players and draft choices unless Wayne would sign a new contract and commit for two years."

As a first step toward a trade, L.A. gave the Rangers permission to talk to Gretzky about a contract. But Gretzky had doubts about going to New York. At the time, the Rangers, who won the Cup in 1994, were playing well, and if New York failed to go all the way after adding him, Gretzky figured he would take the blame. But while he was mulling over his options with New York, Mike Keenan, the coach and general manager of the St. Louis Blues, jumped in and gave the Kings three prospects and two draft choices for Gretzky, confident he could sign the Great One to a new contract before he became a free agent on July 1.

His confidence turned out to be misplaced. After the Blues beat the Toronto Maple Leafs in the opening round of the playoffs, they lost the first two games of the next series to the heavily favored Detroit Red Wings. "I was singled out by Mike [Keenan] as the guy who lost Game 2," Gretzky recalls. "I could handle that. That's part of his responsibility as coach, to motivate guys. But that same night, Jack Quinn, the team president, called my agent, Mike Barnett, and took the Blues' contract offer [a reported $21 million for three years] off the table. The money had already been agreed to. We were just discussing the length of the deferred payments and the interest. You want to play for people who believe in you. If that's all the faith they had in me – to take a deal off the table after one bad game – right then I decided I would never sign with the Blues, which I'd had every intention of doing. Heck, I'd already put down $9,000 for four season tickets to the Cardinals."

Keenan apologized to Gretzky for his outburst, and the Blues came back to win three of the next four games against Detroit. They finally lost to the Red Wings in double over-time in Game 7. Gretzky's inspired play was a big reason St. Louis nearly pulled off the upset, and his stats in the playoffs – two goals and 14 assists in 13 games – were not exactly those of someone ready to contemplate the sunset from a rocking chair. Gretzky loved playing on a line with his pal Brett Hull, but the damage to his pride had been done. "My wife's from St. Louis, and every two or three days for the next two months she'd ask me, 'Are you going to sign again with the Blues?'" Gretzky says. "I'm the type of guy who changes his mind every other day about whether I hate golf or not. But I gave her the same answer every time: 'No way.'"

Smith called Gretzky on July 2, and two weeks later they agreed on a deal. "As much as I've done offensively, I know that to win championships, you need defense," Gretzky says. "The Rangers have great defense. Playing with Brian Leetch was obviously part of the attraction. He reminds me of Paul Coffey [the Oilers' brilliant offensive defenseman during their championship years]. And, of course, I really enjoy playing with Mark. He hasn't changed. Mess wears his heart on his sleeve, just as he always did. The only dif-ference is he's in New York now. He was a hidden jewel in

Edmonton because I overshadowed him, but he was such a team player, the most unselfish player I've played with. It rubbed off on the whole team."

Those who worry that Gretzky will have difficulty adjusting to playing on a team that, for the first time in his career, is not *his* team don't understand his relationship with Messier. Gretzky may have been captain in Edmonton, but Messier led in the locker room. "I never felt I was playing in his shadow," Messier says. "I had a responsibility on the team that was different from Wayne's. Everyone had his role, and I felt great about mine. So did many others about theirs. If we won, and won often, we knew that everyone would get respect. It was only the perception from the outside that the Oilers were Wayne's team or the Rangers are my team."

Make no mistake, though, the Rangers are Messier's team. "That's how it should be," Gretzky says, professing to be looking forward to getting the C off his shirt, if for no better reason than that he can tell reporters to "ask the captain" if they inquire about a lineup change or some other team-related topic that he doesn't want to discuss. "My responsibility here is to take some of the burden off Mark," says Gretzky. "He won't face the top defensive center on the other team every night."

Nor will Gretzky, for that matter. "Wayne's looking forward to not being the only go-to guy on the team, which is what he's been the last couple of years," says Smith, who envisions Gretzky playing with the Rangers' two speedy Russian forwards, 23-year-old Alexei Kovalev and 32-year-old Sergei Nemchinov. "In the best of times Wayne was never fast, so you need to put him with guys who are quick."

That would seem to preclude pairing Gretzky with slow-footed 30-year-old forward Luc Robitaille, his onetime Kings teammate. When Robitaille, who scored 63 goals for Los Angeles in 1992–93, was traded from the Kings to the Pittsburgh Penguins in 1994, he blamed Gretzky for orchestrating the deal, an accusation Gretzky has denied. There was tension between Robitaille and Gretzky after that, but whatever difficulties they had appear to be gone. Smith has talked to both of them about it, and they have assured him that everything has been smoothed over. Furthermore, Messier has guaranteed there won't be friction. "I like Luc," Messier says. "When he wasn't scoring last year, he still went above the call of duty in terms of effort. That's the most important thing to me."

If Messier likes Robitaille, the case is closed as far as Gretzky is concerned. Messier and Gretzky spent lots of time together during the World Cup – playing golf, dining, talking in the locker room, where their cubicles were next to each other – in part so Messier could bring Gretzky up to speed on what was going on with the Rangers and what to expect in New York. "Nothing's for free in New York," Messier says. "You have to bring your A game every night."

There's still no one who sees the ice and passes the puck better than Gretzky – though Pittsburgh's Mario Lemieux is on a par with him – and with the Great One anchoring one power-play unit and Messier another, the Rangers should have one of the most potent special teams in hockey. But whatever Gretzky's on-ice contributions this season, his turn in the Big Apple will add an important dynamic to an already talented Rangers team. "Wayne attracts attention wherever he goes," Messier says. "He's fun to be around.

As a teammate you feed off that energy. The guys will feed off it. I call it catching the wave. That's what gets a team through a season, feeding off each other's energy. Wayne's always going for records, there's a full house every game. It's like a carnival atmosphere around him."

So whoop it up, New Yorkers. The carnival won't last forever. This season and maybe the next one, too, should be a fine, fast ride. "I have great memories of Edmonton," says Messier. "But you always try to make new headlines, new stories. Wayne and I are not the same people as we were when we were 22. But what's new is what's exciting. What's about to happen."

Gretzky's reunion with Messier was a success for the Rangers. He continued to score over a point a game in the 1996–97 season, helping New York to land a playoff berth.

STILL GOING GREAT

BY AUSTIN MURPHY | MAY 5, 1997

At the age of 36, Wayne Gretzky and Mark Messier revived their old magic to lead New York over Florida in the Stanley Cup playoffs

(Photograph by Damian Strohmeyer)

WERE YOU GUILTY TOO? HAD YOU BEGUN TO THINK OF Wayne Gretzky as the Great One Emeritus? Did you think it was time to put Mark (Moose) Messier out to pasture?

Think again. In successive games last week Gretzky and Messier of the New York Rangers covered themselves in glory, and in so doing covered the Florida Panthers with a white sheet, eliminating last season's Eastern Conference champions four games to one in their first-round playoff series. There was Gretzky, celebrating his 58th career hat trick in Game 4 in New York, followed two nights later by Messier's two-goal, three-point eruption in Florida. Note to both 36-year-old former Edmonton Oilers: Forgive us for suspecting that you were no longer capable of such heroics.

We stand corrected and a bit confused. Is this 1997 or 1987? Was that Madison Square Garden Gretzky captivated in Game 4, scoring three times in a span of 6:23 in a 3–2 Rangers win, or was it Northlands Coliseum?

Wherever he has traveled in his illustrious 18-year NHL career, Gretzky has amazed his teammates and coaches not just with his ability to amass points but also with his ability to remember the plays that produced them. His recall is also excellent when it comes to slights, which he harbors and uses as fuel. In this way, says Rangers winger Luc Robitaille, Gretzky is like Michael Jordan. "Say something [critical] about him, he scores 50 points. He's telling you to shut up." Whatever Gretzky was telling us with his play in this series, his voice went from a whisper to a scream.

Pilloried, along with Messier, in the New York press for being all but invisible in a 3–0 Game 1 loss to the Panthers, Gretzky scored the winning goal in Game 2. In silencing some critics, however, he gave others reason to mock. Game 2 was telecast on Fox, whose much-despised FoxTrax puck – which contains a computer chip that highlights the puck on television – must reach 65 mph before it will change from blue to red on your TV screen. Gretzky's change-up goal failed to achieve that velocity, and for several days his teammates teased him for scoring a "blue goal."

Because of a scheduling conflict at Madison Square Garden, Games 3 and 4 had to be played on successive nights, which many observers saw as a looming disaster for the home team. "Two games in two nights? We had no chance," says New York general manager Neil Smith, acidly parroting the pre-Game 3 story line. "It was the old, decrepit, Geritol-swilling Rangers against the virile, young, fleet-footed Panthers."

There seemed to be good reason for the skepticism. All season New York had been maddeningly inconsistent. The Rangers finished fifth in the conference (38–34–10), and with their lack of depth and youth, they were not regarded as serious threats to win the Stanley Cup. Their disciplined, physical play in the first round, however, has prompted a hasty reassessment. In Mike Richter they have a goaltender capable of confounding anyone. In Brian Leetch they have the finest offensive defenseman in the game. And in Gretzky and Messier they have two forces of nature who have found their A games at the right time.

They're still plenty old. But so far this postseason, that hasn't mattered. Before New York eked out a victory in Game 3 – Robitaille tied it with 18.9 seconds left on assists from Gretzky and Messier, and Esa Tikkanen won it with a blur of a slap shot in overtime – the conventional wisdom was that the Rangers *had* to win that one, because youth and fresh legs were sure to prevail less than 24 hours later in Game 4.

Oddly, one of the oldest players in the Garden last Wednesday was the one with the most hop. While younger men wilted, "Wayne was asking for more ice time," said New York coach Colin Campbell. The Rangers put in 23 flat, uninspired minutes before Gretzky started playing as if he had stepped out of a time machine.

None of his three goals would have been a "blue goal," and each was prettier than the last. For goal number 1, he one-timed a feed from Leetch into a yawning net. After his second score, a rocket into the right corner of the top shelf, Gretzky skated to the bench, where Messier said something to him that made him smile. "Keep sniffing," advised the captain.

Thus was a tradition revived. In their salad days as Oilers, whenever Gretzky had two goals in a game Messier would tell him to "keep sniffing" for the hat trick. That's exactly what Gretzky did, and his third goal evoked the Great One at his greatest. Out-manned after carrying the puck into the right side of the Florida zone, he slammed on the brakes, then circled to virtually the same spot. He faked a shot – by now he was toying with Panthers goalie John Vanbiesbrouck – then edged slightly to his left, allowing a screen to form between him and the goaltender. Only then did Gretzky rip a shot that caromed off the left post and in. As Florida coach Doug McLean spat out his gum in disgust, the Great One danced a brief, un-Gretzky-like jig to celebrate his first hat trick in four years.

Inspired by his best friend's heroism, Messier nearly duplicated the feat two nights later. When Messier arrived at Miami Arena before Game 5, he wore the arresting mask his teammates refer to as The Look. "He had it early," said Gretzky, who had shared a cab with Tikkanen and Messier after the Rangers' Friday-morning skate. "Tikk and I were trying to have a conversation, but Mark wasn't participating."

On this day, The Look meant "Look Out, Carkner." After drilling Panthers' defenseman Terry Carkner with a hard check early in his first shift, Messier scored on a breakaway 39 seconds into the game. He scored again with 16 seconds left in the second period and set up Tikkanen's series winner in overtime.

The 32-year-old Tikkanen, a gap-toothed, gimpy-kneed Finn with a bad body and a barely decipherable polylingual dialect, is another former Oiler. His second game-winning goal of the series gave Edmonton East about a week to recuperate before starting the conference semis.

Not that the Rangers need the rest.

The Rangers faced the Devils in the next round, beating them four games to one. They would lose the conference final to the Philadelphia Flyers. During the summer, Mark Messier signed as a free agent with the Vancouver Canucks, ending the reunion with Gretzky. The 1996-97 playoffs were Gretzky's last postseason appearance.

ONE OF A KIND

BY E.M. SWIFT | APRIL 26, 1999

After 21 seasons as the world's greatest hockey player and his sport's greatest ambassador, the incomparable Wayne Gretzky called it quits

(Photograph by David E. Klutho)

HE WAS CERTAIN. YOU COULD SEE IT IN HIS EYES, NOW clear and bright, though an hour earlier, as he took a final lap around the Madison Square Garden ice, they'd been brimming with tears. You could hear it in his voice as he described the phone calls he'd received that morning from Michael Jordan and Mario Lemieux telling him how much he'd enjoy his retirement. You could read it on his face as he described the final timeout that New York Rangers coach John Muckler called with 30 seconds left in a 1–1 game, while the sellout crowd chanted his name. "He called me over and told me, 'Wayne, I found out I had a grandson today. You've got to get me the game-winner.' When I was younger, I might have. But it wasn't to be."

When he was younger, he would have. The Great One's magnetic north had always pointed toward the dramatic, and he'd made a career out of shining brightest when the most eyes were on him. Instead, on Sunday it was the Pittsburgh Penguins' Jaromir Jagr who scored the game-winner in overtime, temporarily putting a damper on number 99's retirement party. But that didn't last long. Gretzky, hugging Jagr, said it was fitting that "the best young player in the game" had scored the winning goal, a sort of passing of the torch. Then Gretzky went to center ice, and before an assemblage of former foes, teammates and friends who'd come to New York for his send-off – Lemieux, Mark Messier, Paul Coffey, Glen Sather, Glenn Anderson, Ulf Samuelsson among them – soaked in a throat-choking 15-minute ovation given by 18,200 fans who'd come to see hockey's greatest player leave the ice for the final time.

Not even taking his skates off later – something Gretzky had been dreading after 21 years of pro hockey – was as hard as he'd feared. Golfer Mark O'Meara, a friend of Gretzky's, happened to choose that moment to come into the Rangers' locker room, and he handed Gretzky a new set of spikes. "That kind of took the edge off it," Gretzky said. "This is a great game, but it's a hard game. Time does something to you, and it's time."

It was a decision he'd been wrestling with since around Christmas, which is when he first brought the subject up with his wife, Janet. This season Gretzky again led the Rangers in scoring (nine goals and 53 assists in 70 games), but his numbers were way down from his usual output, and he had the worst plus-minus rating (minus–23) on the team. Even after winning his third All-Star Game MVP award in Tampa three months ago, Gretzky thought about retirement more and more. While sitting out 12 games in late February and March with an injured disk in his neck, he made up his mind. During his absence the Rangers, who have missed the playoffs two years in a row, went 6–3–3 and played some of their best hockey of the season.

On any given night Gretzky was still capable of thrilling even the most jaded observer with his uncanny passing, but he'd lost too much foot speed. "We were watching a tape at home the other night," he told SI a few hours before his final game. He was relaxed and enjoying his final hours as a pro athlete, autographing pictures and programs and some of the 40 sticks he would use against the Penguins that afternoon. His father, Walter, had come with him to the dressing room and was pouring himself some coffee. His Rangers teammates were beginning to drift in. "My wife said, 'Boy, you were really quick.' I always used to play up how slow I was, but if there was an opening, my first step to the net was as quick as anyone's, and there weren't too many guys who beat me to loose pucks. [Former teammate] Ken Linseman used to say he'd hit me over the head if he heard me say I was slow one more time."

At 38, though, Gretzky was seeing those loose pucks go to younger legs, and his fierce pride told him it was better to leave the game a year early than a year late. Once he'd decided to retire, he didn't announce anything, not wanting to distract the team in its attempt to make the playoffs. He certainly didn't want a grand farewell tour. Gretzky told only Janet and his mother, Phyllis. He couldn't bring himself to confide in Walter, who'd taught him the game on their backyard rink, until a couple of days before his official announcement last Friday. "I knew it would devastate him because it sort of meant he was retiring, too," Wayne said. "I always said I'd be the first one to know when it was time to go, and once I was sure, I didn't want everyone trying to talk me out of it. I never wavered, though my wife put up a good fight until the 11th hour."

It's difficult to overstate Gretzky's impact on the game. He is both hockey's greatest scorer and its greatest ambassador, the man who almost single-handedly made the NHL viable in California, which now has three teams, with his headline-grabbing trade from the Stanley Cup champion Edmonton Oilers to the Los Angeles Kings in 1988. He leaves the game with a mind-numbing 61 NHL records, many of which will never be broken. Scoring patterns in the NHL have changed so dramatically since he was tearing apart the league in the 1980s that some of his numbers seem to come from a different sport. During the six seasons from 1981–82 through 1986–87, Gretzky *averaged* 203 points per year. What was he doing, bowling? No other NHL player has ever scored 200 points.

His record of 92 goals in an 80-game season, which he accomplished in 1981–82, is "unreachable," in the view of Boston Bruins general manager Harry Sinden, who scoffs at the once-popular notion that Gretzky didn't have an outstanding shot. "The Russians used to describe people as short-, medium- and long-range scorers," Sinden says. "Gretzky didn't score on long shots. But he was a scorer from short and medium range because he was so accurate and quick. How about the ones he used to bounce in off the goalie? The first time I saw him do that, I thought it was an accident. But it was a play of his. That's a great shot."

But Gretzky admits, with a rueful smile, that even though he scored 894 goals, the most in NHL history, "10 years from now they won't even talk about my goal scoring; it'll just be my passing."

That was his genius. Gretzky's vision and imagination were such that he routinely created plays no one had ever seen. He played hockey like a chess master, several steps ahead of everyone else. Teammates learned to get open and be ready because Gretzky would find a way to get the puck on their sticks. If it meant banking a pass off the net – another move he perfected – so be it. "No one will ever be able to pass the puck flat all the time the way he did," says Lemieux, who played on a line with Gretzky during the 1987 Canada Cup and credits Gretzky with teaching him what it takes to be a winner. "Practicing with him for six weeks showed me how hard you have to work to be No. 1 in the world."

If Gretzky had never scored a goal, he'd still be the NHL's alltime leading scorer on the strength of his 1,963 assists (the last one came during his finale on Sunday), a staggering 861 more than Coffey, his closest pursuer. Other records that seem secure are his 50 goals in 39 games in 1981–82, his 163 assists in 1985–86 and his DiMaggio-like scoring streak of at least one point in 51 consecutive games in 1983–84.

John Muckler, who first coached Gretzky in Edmonton – where he was the centerpiece of a young, dynamic team that won four Stanley Cups between 1984 and 1988 – stood in the bowels of Madison Square Garden a few hours before Sunday's game looking as if he were preparing for a wake. "Gretz seems to be the only one at ease with this," Muckler said of the retirement. "I tried desperately to talk him out of it. He's been an ambassador, a friend and a great player. The greatest of all time. There'll never be another one."

It's the man, not the record breaker, that the NHL will most miss. He is the sport's only transcendent star and, thanks to those years in L.A., its only link to glamour. But his deep love of the game is still farmboy-simple. The gift Gretzky's New York teammates gave him at his final practice last Saturday said nothing of his records or accomplishments. It was a leather sofa in the shape of a baseball mitt, with a brass plaque at the base bearing the message THANK YOU FOR YOUR PASSION.

"His passion to be the best player in the world is what drove him," says Mike Keenan, who coached Gretzky in the 1987 and 1991 Canada Cups and during Gretzky's brief stint with the St. Louis Blues in 1996. "He never had a game where afterward you could say, 'Wayne looked a little flat tonight.' He was like Michael Jordan that way. He was also one of the most respectful players I've ever coached. He got that from his father."

Wayne got a lot from Walter, a retired Bell Canada telephone employee whose admonitions to Wayne when he was a youngster helped guide him throughout his career. It was eerie, almost as if Walter had foreseen exactly what would become of his son and was grooming him for the role. One life-defining lesson, which Wayne recounted for SI on the morning of his final game, came when he was 10, the year he scored 378 goals in 68 games for a youth team in his hometown of Brantford, Ont.

It was April, and the season was over, but Brantford had scheduled an exhibition game against a small-town team outside Toronto as a fundraiser. Wayne was already famous in hockey-mad Canada – he was nicknamed the Great One in a newspaper article when he was nine – and as usual the arena was packed with adults curious to see this wunderkind. Wayne's mind, for once, was elsewhere. "I loved baseball as much as hockey in those days," he recalled. "My dream was to pitch for the Detroit Tigers. I wanted to play baseball [that day]. Obviously I stunk in the exhibition, because we lost 8–1. Afterward, my father said, 'I don't ever want to see you do that again. All these people came to see you play. You have to be at your top level every night, whether it's a September exhibition or Game 7 of the playoffs.' I always remembered that. I knew I was on display."

That was true off the ice and on. The responsibility that went with Wayne's talent was another thing Walter drilled home. Like his boyhood idol, Gordie Howe, Gretzky was uncommonly willing to sign autographs, unusually accommodating with the media (especially in the new markets into which the NHL was expanding in the South and West) and unfailingly polite. "He was the highest-profile player in the league his entire career, and I don't think he ever made a mistake," says Sinden. "When your best player is like that, it has an effect on everyone in the game. Not just the young guys. Even a person like me. I don't think Wayne Gretzky ever did anything that wasn't for the betterment of the game."

"I think the worst thing he did was refer to the [New Jersey] Devils as a Mickey Mouse organization," says Detroit Red Wings coach Scotty Bowman. "He was the kind of guy who'd get to know the clubhouse people, the stick-boys. He treated everyone with respect. With older people, it was always Mister. I'd say, 'It's Scotty.' But it was always Mr. Bowman. Even now. It's just the way he was raised."

People talk about the burden of potential, but for Gretzky it was never a burden. He loved the challenge of having to live up to high expectations. Even as a teenager he had no problem with being compared with the great players of the past. He knew how good he was. When he was 16, the year he used number 99 for the first time because number 9 (which had been worn by both Howe and Bobby Hull) wasn't available, he was asked if it was a Howe 99 or a Hull 99. "That's a Gretzky 99" was his reply. (It is, too. The NHL retired the number on Sunday.)

When he heard someone say he was too small, too young or too slow, he relished proving his detractor wrong. "My peers were calling me the Great One, the next Bobby Orr," he recalled on Sunday. "But when I was 16, 75% of the people said I'd never play in the NHL. That pushed me to greater heights. 'That's an opinion I'm going to change,' I'd say to myself. I shocked a lot of people when I came to the NHL."

The thinking in 1979–80, Gretzky's rookie season in the NHL, was that the 18-year-old hotshot from the World Hockey Association, lacking size (he was 5'11" and weighed 170 pounds), speed and toughness, would get killed. It was a much more violent league then – the Philadelphia Flyers, a.k.a. the Broad Street Bullies, were the NHL's top draw – with few European players. A few tough hits, some observers thought, would slow the kid down.

Only no one could touch him. Quick, unpredictable and elusive, Gretzky ushered in a new style of play that spelled the doom of the big, tough, immobile defenseman. "He was able to turn on a dime like no one else," says Lemieux.

"There are few teams and few individuals who made the game different," says Florida Panthers president Bill Torrey, who watched Gretzky's Oilers end the dynasty of his New York Islanders in 1984 and start one of their own. "Gretzky and the Oilers did. Their all-out attack was something the league had not seen before. They had a lot of great players, but Gretzky was the pin-wheel, the way Orr was the pinwheel for those great Bruins teams. They just blew people away. The game opened up, and Gretzky was the catalyst."

"He was more European in his style than North American," says Bowman. "He used quick counterattacks, which is how he got so many breakaways. Edmonton also used him as a penalty killer. Very few offensive stars had been used in that role before. Now nearly every team does it."

He had two signature moves. Gretzky would set up behind the net – the Rangers painted 99 behind both goals on Sunday in his honor – from which point he would feed breaking wingers or, if left unchallenged, dart out in front for a wrap-around. (Once, Muckler recalled on Sunday, Gretzky used a third option: getting the puck flat onto his stick blade and, lacrosse-style, firing it into the goal off the back of Blues goalie Mike Liut, one of five goals he tallied in a 1981 game.)

Gretzky's second innovation was to break over the blue line and spin toward the boards, eventually passing to a teammate who broke late into the zone. "For many years the modus operandi in the league was to headman the puck, but Gretzky changed that," says Sinden. "He was the first one to make the late man coming into the zone – usually Coffey or Jari Kurri – the most dangerous man. Gretzky could hold onto the puck for so long, turning toward the boards and stickhandling in place, that even if you knew what he was going to do, you couldn't stop him."

This went on for years. On Sunday, Gretzky used the spinorama play a half-dozen times, nearly always creating a scoring chance. Yet even to someone sitting high in the stands, where the patterns of play are clearer, Gretzky's passes were surprising. They brought a collective gasp of delight as they found the open men. It all left you longing for more.

Which was, after all, the point. Gretzky's timing has always been surpassing, and his retirement party – he wanted the two days between the announcement on Friday and his last game to have the feel of a party – showed he hadn't lost his touch. He raised the bar on sports retirements. "This is not a passing on, it's a moving on," he told a friend, saying he was going to take a long time away from hockey to enjoy himself and to enjoy being a parent to his three kids: 10-year-old Paulina, eight-year-old Ty and six-year-old Trevor. Then, who knows? "I really believe he'll be involved in ownership," Muckler says. "He'll be back."

It's hard to feel bad for Gretzky. His is one career for which there'll be no following acts. Ninety-nine was one of a kind.

Gretzky retired as the greatest player of all time, and remains so to this day. In over a decade since, no one has even come close to his single-season points, goals or assists records. His career totals remain just as untouchable; the second place alltime scorer (Mark Messier) has fewer total points than Gretzky has assists alone.

THE GREAT ONES

BY MICHAEL FARBER | MARCH 4, 2002

*Wayne Gretzky's handpicked team gave Canada the gold it
craved in a tournament that showcased hockey at its best*

(Photograph by David E. Klutho)

THE FIRST RULE IN JOURNALISM IS TO FOLLOW THE MONEY, which brings us to that now famous coin that was embedded at center ice before the start of the Olympic hockey tournament. It was a Canadian one-dollar piece, popularly called a loonie. (That's because there is an image of a loon on it, not because it has dropped 35% against the U.S. dollar in the past 10 years.) This good-luck loonie was surreptitiously implanted by an Edmontonian named Dan Craig, the NHL ice technician who was moonlighting at the Salt Lake City Games. The coin was dug up after the gold medal game on Sunday and handed to Team Canada executive director Wayne Gretzky, who elevated it to artifact and will give it to the Hockey Hall of Fame in Toronto, passing the buck for the first time in his life.

The final score was Canada 5, USA 2, NBC 10.7. There were 38 million homes in the U.S. tuned in to a fitting final of an extraordinary tournament, the most for a hockey game since the 1980 Miracle on Ice. The overnight ratings were spectacular compared with the microscopic numbers the sport usually generates in the U.S. (ABC's average rating for last season's Stanley Cup finals was 3.3.) However, the numbers that count, as hockey continues the battle to establish itself as something more than NASCAR of the North, will be the ones that emerge over the next 20 years, when kids who watched the gold medal game start playing and become involved in the sport.

The first Olympic tournament played by pros that could be seen by Americans who weren't insomniacs or night watchmen might prove to be a watershed moment for the sport – and for North America – which prompted Owen Nolan to bolt the Team Canada bench with four minutes to go, race into the dressing room and grab his video camera. Nolan, a right wing with some jump and a lot of zoom, recorded a moment that will forever resonate across a country that had been starved for Olympic gold for half a century. (When asked what he would have done if coach Pat Quinn had called for his line to play in the final minute, Nolan said, "I wasn't going.") The ambient noise on the tape was a spontaneous chorus of *O Canada* that shook the E Center in the final 45 seconds of hockey's best, if not last, chance to showcase its top-of-the-line wares internationally.

This was a day for Canada to puff out its chest – "What sets us apart is our determination and heart; I'd take 20 Canadian guys from the NHL and nine times out of 10 win the Stanley Cup," forward Theo Fleury said after the final – but the warm postgame handshakes and hugs between the Canadian and U.S. players were a reminder that within 48 hours they would again be Red Wings, Flyers and Rangers. The 32 players in the gold medal game who were facing a teammate are now answering the siren call of dollars. But in two-hour games over 10 furious days, hockey put aside money (not to mention fighting, scrums after whistles and filibusters that masquerade as face-offs) in a series of compelling matches that captivated a usually indifferent viewing public.

Question: Could thrilling Olympic hockey be replicated in the NHL?

Answer: Absolutely, as long as the 30-team NHL contracts by 24 clubs, reduces its schedule from six months to two weeks, holds one-game playoff series and finds a way to incorporate national pride into the games.

The Olympic tournament did many things – it assuaged Canada's damaged pride, erased memories of the ugly on-ice play and off-ice conduct by the Americans in Nagano and established the Swedes, who were shocked by Belarus in the quarterfinals, as the greatest choke artists since Isadora Duncan got her scarf caught in the car's rear wheel – but it can't be a blueprint for Phoenix Coyotes–Tampa Bay Lightning games. It is foolish to compare the Olympics, which features fourth-liners who are bona fide stars, with the quotidian schedule of a 700-player league. The NHL should, and will, swipe some of the ideas from the Olympic tournament, starting with the hurry-up face-off rule and perhaps no-touch icing if, as one NHL general manager put it, the league is willing to lose "the race car effect" of players crashing into the end boards in pursuit of a loose puck. NHL games will be played with more dispatch in coming seasons, but $125 rinkside seats won't be removed to expand the ice surface to Olympic size (15 feet wider than NHL arenas), the three 100-second TV timeouts per period won't disappear, and despite a growing sentiment among players, including Mario Lemieux, that removing the red line would enhance the flow of the game, this is a back-burner issue.

"Having no red line would be like eliminating the running game from football," says NHL executive vice president Colin Campbell. The elimination of a red line proved to be a red herring at the Olympics because Team Canada and Team USA often acted as if it really were in play, rejecting the impulse to go deep and sticking primarily to zone-to-zone passes, playing a familiar brand of small hockey that effectively shrunk the international rink. The Canadians were slower learners than the U.S. but ultimately developed the necessary patience to make plays. Foremost was the pass Steve Yzerman whipped cross-ice to Jarome Iginla, who shoveled the puck past U.S. goalie Mike Richter, giving Canada a late two-goal, third-period lead and sending Nolan for his camera.

Gretzky rose from his seat and pumped his arms in triumph at Iginla's goal, a stunning turnaround from six days earlier, when the greatest ambassador in hockey resigned his diplomatic portfolio. After a 3–3 tie against the Czech Republic that completed the round-robin portion of the tournament, Gretzky entered a press conference and unloaded. Troubled by rumors that Lemieux would have to go home with an injured hip and that his coaches were at philosophical loggerheads, Gretzky blasted "American propaganda" and said the Europeans hate Canada and want to beat it worse than Canada wants to beat them. That pretty much covered the known hockey world.

This was paranoia with a purpose, a gimmick Gretzky learned from his former Edmonton Oilers coach and general manager, Glen Sather. The outburst, which Gretzky repeated the following day, rallied fainthearted fans at home, diverted attention from a team that had yet to beat a quality opponent and stole the newspaper headlines in a country that treats hockey with an aching earnestness. "It always matters more in Canada," says Tom Poti, the U.S. defenseman who plays for the Oilers. "That's pretty much what they've got."

The Americans were working on their own stories in the relative privacy of their practices. Coach Herb Brooks's mantra was, "Write your own script. Write your own story." At practice the day before the semifinal against Russia, Brooks threw a pen at the feet of left wing John LeClair, saying, "Johnny, write your own story." With a tournament-high six goals LeClair was telling a story better than LeCarré.

The ideal coach in 1980, uniting a team of college kids and sending them out to beat the world, Brooks remained the ideal coach 22 years later, prodding hard-bitten pros with homilies and buzzwords such as "rebound." During a team meeting Brooks asked his players how many games there were in the NHL season. "Eighty-two," Mike Modano replied confidently.

"Do you agree, John?" Brooks said, wheeling on LeClair.

"I'm going to say no," LeClair said, "because I think you want something else."

Brooks said the correct answer was one game 82 times, a reminder not to look beyond the task at hand. Last Friday the U.S. could hardly look ahead when the entire world was looking back: Twenty-two years to the day after the Miracle on Ice at Lake Placid, the Russians and the U.S. were playing in another Olympic semifinal. The comparison was illuminating.

First, this was Russia, not the Soviet Union. Two of Russia's players, Sergei Fedorov and Darius Kasparaitis, were U.S. citizens, and another, Igor Larionov, was a Canadian citizen whose daughters, Alyonka and Dianna, sometimes sing the U.S. national anthem at Detroit Red Wings games. Russian coach Slava Fetisov even used a few English terms – reverse, forecheck, D-to-D – when he talked to his team of NHL players.

After the U.S. withstood a furious third-period Russian rally in a 3–2 win so intense that it left the Americans running on fumes two days later in the final, Fedorov gave Red Wings teammate Brett Hull a congratulatory pat on the rump. This was about hockey, not the passport, a point Jeremy Roenick of the U.S. tried to make on the eve of the gold medal game when he noted, "My favorite player is Steve Yzerman, and he's Canadian."

A reporter pointed out that Yzerman had received U.S. citizenship. "Well," said a nonplussed Roenick, "the U.S. is the greatest country in the world, but Canada is a close second."

The closeness continued at the highest levels of the game when NHL commissioner Gary Bettman, NHL Players' Association director Bob Goodenow and International Ice Hockey Federation president Rene Fasel hunkered down last Thursday in a four-man bobsled for a trip down the

Olympic course at slap-shot speed. The fate of NHL players returning to the Olympics four years from now in Turin, Italy, is in their white-knuckled hands. They have different constituencies – Bettman has 30 owners, Goodenow has 700 players, Fasel has 63 hockey-playing countries – and the agendas sometimes clash.

In a real-life game of rock-paper-scissors Fasel refuses to allow the Olympic preliminary matches to be played in September, before the NHL season, or to shorten the tournament to fewer than 16 days. Bettman insists the NHL can't afford to lose its momentum by shutting down its season for more than 12 days, although NHL involvement in 2006 would probably require a minimum of two weeks. Goodenow might not be amenable to a format like the one the IIHF used for its eight-team women's Olympic tournament, which was played in 10 days by eliminating four teams after the round-robin round and going straight to the semifinals. "We are driven by passion [for hockey]," Fasel said last week. "They are driven by profit."

Given the artistic success of Salt Lake City, it seems loony not to find a way to make it work.

Gretzky reprised his role as Team Canada's executive director for the 2006 Olympics in Turin, though the success of 2002 would not be repeated as Canada finished out of medal contention. At the 2010 Olympics in Vancouver, Gretzky had the honor of lighting the Olympic torch.

GREAT TO BE BACK

BY E.M. SWIFT | NOVEMBER 28, 2005

Six years removed from his last shift, Wayne Gretzky brought his superstar luster back to the NHL, coaching the surprising Phoenix Coyotes – and loving it

(Photograph by Robert Beck)

FOREVER A STEP AHEAD, THE GREATEST PLAYER IN hockey history finishes the sentence before it's out of the interviewer's mouth: "...tough enough?" he says. "You didn't know if I was tough enough to coach?" The Great One looks away, a slightly pained expression creasing his still youthful face. He's 44 now. "I wouldn't say [being tough] has been the hard part, but it's not the enjoyable part. I'm here for one thing. The enjoyment is winning. That's where the satisfaction comes from."

He is alive. Behind the Phoenix Coyotes' bench, at practices with a whistle between his teeth, unwinding from a game on a charter at 2 a.m., talking to the press, yelling at the refs, having a cup of coffee with the trainer, teasing his young players in the locker room – Wayne Gretzky's blue eyes now burn with intensity and life. Ever since he took his last NHL shift, on April 18, 1999, with the New York Rangers, something had been missing for the world's richest rink rat.

"It wasn't that he was antsy before [he started coaching], but he was unsettled," says Janet Gretzky, who helped talk her husband into taking the Phoenix job despite the complications of having a home in Los Angeles and five children under age 17. "He likes to throw things at me to see if they'll stick. One day he said, 'Maybe I'll coach.' I said, 'Why not? It seems like a natural thing. Why not give back some of the knowledge you have?' It's the happiest he's been since he retired. When someone's this happy in what they're doing, it's hard not to feel good about it."

His friends see the difference. Bryan Wilson, who coached Gretzky when he was 12, recently visited Phoenix. "I watch you behind the bench," Wilson told Gretzky. "You're living and dying with every pass. Are you liking this?"

"Great, isn't it?" Gretzky said. "I love it."

Most important for the Phoenix franchise, Gretzky's players feel his passion, and they've responded by playing above expectations, going 11–10–2 through Sunday with eight one-goal losses. "People don't realize he's very intense," says veteran forward Mike Ricci, 34, the Coyotes' oldest forward. "It's a quiet intensity, but he's so into it. That's what we all respect."

That and the fact that they are playing for the Great One: the NHL's alltime goals, assists and points leader, winner of four Stanley Cups and holder of 59 scoring records. Coyotes captain Shane Doan grew up in Edmonton watching Gretzky. Doan remembers crying as a six-year-old when the Oilers lost in the finals to the New York Islanders, remembers Gretzky's mind-boggling stats: 92 goals in one season, 163 assists in another. "But Wayne has the ability to disarm people and make them feel relaxed," Doan says. "His love of the game and knowledge of the game is incredible, and he can pass that on because he's a good communicator. He wants to win as much as any of us. It's not fake. That emotion is there."

The common thought, of course, is that great players seldom make great coaches. But here's the reality: Many superstar athletes *don't* communicate well. They aren't patient, detail-oriented and insightful judges of human nature – all requisites for being a successful coach. Gretzky, who has been the Coyotes' managing partner in charge of hockey operations since 2001, has all those traits, as well as humility, which allows him to delegate. He relies on his assistants Barry Smith, Rick Bowness and Rick Tocchet as he learns on the fly. And he is not in this for the short term. "Five years from now I'll be a better coach than I am today," Gretzky says.

"Think about what kind of player he was," says Cliff Fletcher, the Coyotes' VP of hockey operations. "He used to think his way around the ice. That was the source of his success more than his physical attributes, and that transfers into the locker room as a coach."

So why was Fletcher surprised last summer when Gretzky decided to coach the rebuilding Coyotes, who went 22–36–18 in 2003–04? "I wondered why he would subject himself to the criticism," Fletcher says. "What did he have to gain? A lot of his friends were saying the same thing, which I think had something to do with his decision. If you tell him he can't do something, it just motivates him to prove you wrong. It was the same when he was a player."

"People would say, 'You're not going to let him do it, are you?'" says Mike Barnett, Gretzky's longtime agent and the Coyotes' general manager. "I'd say, 'I can't stop him, and I'm not inclined to.' He's doing this for one reason: He wants to. He was looking for something to make him excited to get out of bed every morning."

Gretzky's interest in coaching dates to the late 1990s, when he and Barnett took in a New York Knicks game against the Indiana Pacers, who were then run by Larry Bird. "Up until then people always said you couldn't be a great player and a great coach," says Gretzky. "Bird disproved that."

Afterward Gretzky mentioned that he, too, might enjoy coaching after his playing career. Barnett never heard another word about it until the summer of 2004. With the lockout looming, Gretzky was Team Canada's executive director for the World Cup, the same role he'd filled to great fanfare for Canada's gold-medal-winning team at the Olympics in 2002. Pat Quinn, Wayne Fleming, Ken Hitchcock and Jacques Martin were World Cup coaches – Canada won the tournament – and hanging around them, Gretzky got the coaching bug. "I saw that their work ethic, preparation and desire was just like the player's" Gretzky says. "I saw the enjoyment they had. I thought, I want to be part of something like that."

In addition to his Team Canada duties, he'd been playing golf during the lockout, doing corporate outings, watching hours of classic hockey games on TV. "People ask me, 'Do you miss playing?'" Gretzky says. "It *kills* me that I can't play. I remember exactly where I was when I decided to retire. We were playing in Edmonton and Calgary in February of 1999. I'd been on a bus, and my back was so sore, my arm had gone numb. After both those games I stayed on the bench an extra few minutes. I knew it was over.

"Coaching is the closest thing to being a player. Even if you've put a team together, once the game starts, you have no bearing on the outcome. It's out of your hands. The first time I had the feeling I had as a player was my first game as a coach."

Quinn, the coach of the Toronto Maple Leafs, saw hints of Gretzky's ability to lead at the World Cup. "He helps people feel important about what is happening, and that is real leadership," says Quinn. "It's not about him, and it's all about the group. There's no deception or b.s. in him. I don't think that the downside – *Boy, I could look bad out of this thing* – would ever cross his mind. He thinks about the opportunities."

Why *would* Gretzky think about the downside of coaching a team that hasn't won a playoff series since moving from Winnipeg to Phoenix in 1996? Whether it was turning pro at the unprecedented age of 17, leading a former WHA team to four Stanley Cups, single-handedly making hockey a hot ticket in L.A. or overseeing Canada's 2002 Olympic effort when anything less than the country's first hockey gold in 50 years would have been considered failure, Gretzky has always risen to a challenge.

"I was at this year's Kentucky Derby, talking to Pat Riley at a friend's house, and he was very encouraging to me," Gretzky says. "He talked about how much satisfaction he'd had coaching. I always thought he and Glen Sather [Gretzky's coach at Edmonton] were similar in the way they reenergized and refocused their best players every year. The Lakers of the 1980s were Showtime, run-and-gun, like our Oilers, and Riley pushed his best players really hard. So did Slats. If you get your best players to perform at an elite level, everything else falls into place."

After Mike Comrie, one of Phoenix's most talented

forwards, had only three assists in his first nine games, Gretzky made him sit one out. "I explained it to him," Gretzky says. "He was pressing. I wanted him to relax. I've known him since he was three, and I told him, 'No one's trying to take your job away. You can go two ways: Call your agent, sulk and ask to be traded – or prove me wrong.'"

The 25-year-old Comrie responded with three goals and two assists over the next two games. At week's end he was second on the team in scoring.

Only nine players who ended 2003–04 with the Coyotes are still on the roster. While the new rules encourage the wide-open style he favored as a player, the offensive magic Gretzky possessed isn't easily instilled. "That's the hard part," he says. "Behind the net was my forte, but I started working on that when I was 14 and had it down pretty well by 22. You can't expect someone to pick that up at this level. I do tell my centers the less you hold onto the puck, the more effective you'll be. Give-and-go. I very rarely held the puck longer than two seconds. That's one fundamental I really believe in. Working with the young guys, seeing them progress, has been very rewarding.

"You're not going to turn it around in 20 games. I knew I could be patient from coaching my son Trevor's baseball team when they were eight, nine, 10 years old. I tell our guys they're going to make mistakes, they're going to get beat sometimes one-on-one. I'll live with that. What we can't live with is mental mistakes. That's why the second game of the year was so embarrassing."

Against the Kings on Oct. 6 the Coyotes turned in the wrong lineup card, mistakenly listing ace penalty killer Fredrik Sjostrom as a scratch. Just before the opening face-off Sjostrom was ruled ineligible. The Kings scored two power-play goals in a 3–2 win. "I apologized to the team and said it would never happen again," Gretzky says. "Then I called Quinn and Hitchcock and told them not to laugh because they'd done it too."

After the Coyotes started the season 1–4–1, Gretzky showed doubters he had the moxie to make hard decisions. *Tough enough?* When 741-goal scorer Brett Hull, a close friend of Gretzky's, struggled, Gretzky cut Hull's ice time to such a degree that he retired. Gretzky traded center Jeff Taffe, his niece's fiancé, to the Rangers. He made healthy scratches of two of his most experienced players, Ricci and Sean O'Donnell.

Two days after the Coyotes blew leads in losses on Oct. 29 and 30, Gretzky put them through a 50-minute practice without pucks. "We knew it was coming," says Doan. "He's a controlled guy. He doesn't yell and scream. But you know when he's upset. We've also had scrimmages playing wrong-handed, where everyone's laughing. He wants players to enjoy coming to the rink."

Gretzky has found it hardest to integrate his family into his coaching life. His 15-year-old son, Ty, a ninth-grader, lives with him in Phoenix, plays high school hockey and works as a stick boy on the Coyotes' bench. But Paulina, 16, Trevor, 13, Tristan, 5, and Emma, 2, live with Janet in L.A., commuting to Phoenix when the Coyotes are home on weekends – if they can work around Paulina's budding singing career and Trevor's baseball team. "We'll make it work," says Janet. "He's found his niche. We talk after games, and it's upsetting for us after a loss. But he feels he's put everything out there, 120%, just as he did as a player."

"I get emotional," Gretzky says. "Sometimes my heart rate doesn't come down till the morning after a game. But it's enjoyable. I needed this stress, I guess. I needed the challenge. Did I think I was going to like it? Yeah. Did I think I was going to love it? Probably not. But I do. I love it."

Gretzky spent four years as the Coyotes coach, missing the play-offs each year and never posting a winning record. He stepped down as coach in 2009, when the team was sold to the league.

SPORTSMAN OF THE YEAR REVISITED

BY BRIAN CAZENEUVE | DECEMBER 12, 2011

Almost 30 years after being named Sportsman of the Year, Gretzky considers the award and the impact of hockey on his life

(Photograph by Robert Beck)

AN HOUR AFTER PLAYING 18 HOLES ON THE GOLF COURSE
near his house in Westlake Village, Calif., Wayne Gretzky
is decked out in a suit and tie, always prepared to spread
the gospel of his game. Though he hasn't had an official
connection to the NHL since his tenure as coach and part
owner of the Phoenix Coyotes ended in 2009, he is in
many ways still the face of the sport. At 50, hockey's greatest player and ambassador is still on his game, with neither a hair nor a word out of place. "Everything I have I
owe to the game of hockey," he says, in a familiar refrain.
"I never forget it."

He is still revered in Edmonton, where bus route number
99 runs past Wayne Gretzky Drive, but he also owns a restaurant in Toronto, runs a hockey fantasy camp in Las Vegas
and lit the cauldron at the 2010 Winter Olympics in
Vancouver. Some of the proceeds from his Ontario winery
support his foundation that promotes youth hockey. One of
his vintages, a Shiraz-Cabernet blend, has won three gold
medals at the Ontario Wine Awards.

Wayne and his wife, Janet, have five children, ages eight
to 22. Their middle child, Trevor, 19, was drafted by the

Chicago Cubs last June and will play outfield in their minor league system next year.

On being named Sportsman of the Year: "I remember thinking, Wow, I made it, this is pretty cool. So many athletes think about championships and being on winning teams. That's what they should be taught. But being presented that trophy was one of the greatest honors I've ever had. It was one of those awards that I thought, Wow, a hockey player or a guy living in Canada could never win this."

On when he knew he could be an elite player: "Going to the World Junior Championships when I was 16 and playing for Team Canada. And I only made the team because our top two centermen were injured. Once I played in that tournament, that's when I said to everyone, You know what, if I can play against the best 19- and 20-year-olds in the world, I'm going to be a professional hockey player."

On his legacy: "I'm always most proud of when people say, 'I used to love how hard you worked.' I was telling my boys the other day that you know, the greatest athletes in the world have a lot of bad games. The difference is that the greatest athletes, when they have bad games, are still as good or better than the other guys because they work so hard."

On today's game: "There's a little bit less creativity than we had in the 1980s. Everything's more X and O now. It's more defined what each player's role is. But the game is better because the players are better athletes. These guys are fast, they all shoot the puck, they have great reflexes."

On his proudest moments off the ice: "When they asked me to light the Olympic flame, I was so excited and so proud because there were so many people they could have chosen. In my life I've met so many wonderful people and had an opportunity to be involved in charitable work. The Canadian National Institute for the Blind is in my hometown, so I've done a lot of work with blind kids. Because of the NHL, I've had a chance to be a part of helping a lot of people."

On playing versus coaching: "Coaching is wonderful. Would I ever do it again? I don't think so. I loved doing it when I did it. But life goes on. The difference is when you get ready for a game as a player, you get ready yourself. You mentally prepare, you physically get ready, you go through things, what you're going to do. When you're coaching, you've got to get 20 guys to be thinking the exact same way. And every guy doesn't think that way. Every athlete is different."

On the joy of free time: "Because of my job, there were a lot of things I didn't get an opportunity to do. I can go to my kids' school plays, pick them up at school, watch Little League games. I'm around more. My life is way more relaxing now. In hockey it's about winning and losing. It's peaks and valleys. There's no in-between. And now I don't have that. My peaks and valleys are if I shoot 82 or I shoot 88. Is that going to change the world? No. I just have to enjoy myself."

On the future: "I don't know. Maybe my son will make the Cubs. And if something comes along, I'll be back in the NHL. Right now it's not the right time for me. Right now I'm really enjoying being a fan. It's a great game. One day hopefully I'll be back."